Differentiation That Really Works

Grades 6–12

Works

Language Arts

Strategies From Real Teachers for Real Classrooms

Differentiation That Really Works

Grades 6–12

Language Arts

Cheryll M. Adams, Ph.D.,
and Rebecca L. Pierce, Ph.D.

Routledge
Taylor & Francis Group

NEW YORK AND LONDON

First published in 2012 by Prufrock Press Inc.

Published 2021 by Routledge
605 Third Avenue, New York, NY 10017
2 Park Square, Milton Park, Abingdon, Oxon OX14 4RN

Routledge is an imprint of the Taylor & Francis Group, an informa business

Copyright © 2012 by Taylor & Francis Group

Production design by Raquel Trevino

ISBN 13: 978-1-0321-4319-4 (hbk)
ISBN 13: 978-1-5936-3836-8 (pbk)

DOI: 10.4324/9781003234647

Dedication

This book is dedicated to the many teachers and students with whom we have worked in appreciation for what we have learned from them. We also dedicate this book to our families and friends for their love and support.

CONTENTS

ACKNOWLEDGEMENTS

Although there are many who write in the area of differentiation, the thoughts of Carol Tomlinson have been a tremendous influence on our work and practice. We share her passion for supporting teachers as they design learning environments that meet the needs of diverse learners. She has inspired us to seek out teachers who are practicing professionals and have embraced differentiation. The teachers we selected have or are working toward their license in gifted education. It was our privilege to work with them and we appreciate their willingness to share their work. We gratefully acknowledge the following teachers whose contributions are found in this book:

Laura Alexander
Ami Brown
Susan Burson
Jenny Duguid
Amanda Fisher
Chris Gesse
Karrie Hamilton
Suzanne Jones

Rebecca Knight
Stephen Merkle
Jessica Rogers
Quella Rutledge
Lisa Sarjeant
Susan Schweitzer
Tracy Schwerin
Teri Vasquez

CHAPTER 1

INTRODUCTION

Why We Wrote This Book

Many years ago, we were classroom teachers ourselves, and we spent time working with students, trying to understand their needs. We read some of the early work of A. Harry Passow and Sandy Kaplan coming out of the National/State Leadership Training Institute of the 1970s, and thus began our journey toward learning how to differentiate instruction to meet the needs of all of the learners in our classroom. We both found early on in our teaching careers that giving all students the same assignment resulted in some students doing well while others were bored or frustrated. Thus, we learned how to differentiate as a means of surviving and allowing students to thrive. We learned that "more" and "faster" were not better for our gifted students, but that we needed qualitatively different work that centered on broad-based themes, issues, and problems. We learned that, in order to achieve, all of our students required choice and challenge. Now that we have left the precollege classroom and teach at the university level, we still have to differentiate to meet the needs of our undergraduate and graduate students.

Currently, we work together at the Center for Gifted Studies and Talent Development on a number of projects related to differentiated instruction and meeting the needs of learners in the classroom. The center is located in Burris Laboratory School on the campus of Ball State University. The proximity of the center to the Laboratory School provides us the opportunity to work with teachers and students on a regular basis so that we do not lose the important connection to what is actually happening in classrooms today. Working in the Laboratory School and in other schools throughout the United States, we have been able to use our practitioners' and researchers' lens to identify strategies that work well in the classroom.

DOI: 10.4324/9781003234647-1

The strategies that we have chosen to include in this book had to meet several criteria: (1) be easy to implement, (2) be easy to modify, (3) encourage student engagement, (4) have inherent opportunities for differentiation, and (4) be appropriate for multiple grade levels. The strategies we've selected are not an exhaustive list of differentiation strategies, but they are the ones that we see most often being used by real teachers who differentiate well. Although there is little empirical evidence to support the use of these strategies, the practice-based evidence is widespread (Coil, 2007; Gregory & Chapman, 2002; Kingore, 2004; Tomlinson, 2003; Winebrenner, 1992). We think these strategies are vital for teachers to have in their bag of tricks if they want to provide choice and challenge for all learners in their classroom. However, quality differentiating requires more than just a simple bag of tricks.

Working with teachers for more than 14 years nationally and internationally, we found some who were differentiating to a high degree and some who were just beginning to differentiate. We found some who did it well and some who struggled. Comparing and contrasting those teachers who differentiated well from their colleagues who struggled allowed us to zero in on classroom components that seemed to make the difference. What we found is that many teachers were using strategies to differentiate instruction but lacked the management to facilitate multiple groups working on different activities. Others had interesting lessons and activities but when some students finished early, chaos was present. Some teachers differentiated a lesson by providing several paths to reach the same goal, but all students were required to complete the same assessment. Those teachers who had the most successful classrooms not only used differentiated learning strategies but also made use of anchoring activities, classroom management, and differentiated assessment. Realizing that these four components are necessary led to the development of our model, Creating an Integrated Response for Challenging Learners Equitably: A Model by Adams and Pierce (CIRCLE MAP; Adams & Pierce, 2006). We have realized that when teachers have all four components clearly articulated and they implement them, the stage is set for successful differentiation.

We learned something else with our teachers: No matter the level of experience or the effectiveness of differentiation, everyone's issue was time. We have had the privilege to come in contact with teachers who differentiate in their classrooms on a daily basis. These classrooms are "pockets of excellence" where teachers embrace the differentiation mindset and look at everything they do through the differentiation lens. We felt other teachers could gain some time by using lessons that practicing professionals have already created and tested in their own classrooms. The lessons in this book focus on middle and high school language arts and can be used as written or modified to meet the needs of your own language arts classroom. We have provided templates that can be used to develop your own materials using the strategies included here.

How Is This Book Different From Every Other Book on Differentiated Strategies?

This book is different because real teachers designed the lessons. Practicing professionals (everyday classroom teachers in the trenches) tested them in their own heterogeneous classrooms. These professionals differentiate on a regular basis. We have included comments for each lesson from the teacher who developed it, describing how to use the strategy and how his or her students responded to the activity. In addition, on many lessons, we have included comments from other teachers who reacted to it.

How to Use This Book

The following steps should be kept in mind as you make your way through the book:
1. Choose the strategy you want to implement.
2. Look at the sample lessons.
3. Don't be afraid to modify a lesson to fit your grade level and the needs of your own students.
4. Use the template to design your own lesson.
5. Use it in your classroom and enjoy!

CIRCLE MAP Model

What Is Differentiation?

Although its early focus denoted modifying curricula to meet the needs of the gifted and talented (Passow, 1982; Ward, 1980), differentiation has since taken center stage as a means of meeting the needs of academically diverse students in the heterogeneous classroom through modifying the curriculum and learning experiences of these students (Tomlinson, 1999, 2001, 2003). Differentiation is not a collection of strategies; it is not simply offering students choices; it is not group work. Although these options may be found in a differentiated classroom, differentiation involves finding multiple ways to structure learning so that each student has an opportunity to work at a moderately challenging level. It is an organized, yet flexible, way of proactively adjusting teaching and learning to meet students where they are, while helping all students achieve maximum growth as learners (Tomlinson, 1999). Put succinctly, differentiation is a mindset, a lens to use in examining every aspect of the classroom. Instruction may be differentiated in content, process, product, learning environment, and affect according to the students' readiness, interest, or learning profiles. For example, all of the students may be studying force and motion (content), but the laboratory experiments in which they participate may be at varying levels of complexity to accommodate their academic readiness for a particular task (process).

Successful differentiation will occur in the classroom when a number of essential elements also are addressed. These essential elements include specific classroom management techniques that address the special needs of a differentiated classroom through flexible use of time, space, and student groups; planned use of anchoring activities; a variety of differentiated instructional strategies; and differentiated assessment (Adams & Pierce, 2006).

The Model

Having worked with preservice and in-service teachers over the last decade to help implement differentiated instructional strategies in their classrooms, we have noticed several commonalities among teachers who are successful. As a result of this research, we developed the CIRCLE MAP model. The CIRCLE MAP, shown in Figure 1, is appropriate for any grade level and content area. It weaves together four elements—classroom management techniques, anchoring activities, differentiated instructional strategies, and differentiated assessment—that we found as the commonalities among teachers who differentiated successfully. Having observed teachers across the country and internationally, we found these elements consistently in classrooms that addressed the needs of all children. For a complete discussion of the model, see Adams and Pierce (2006).

Our purpose in writing this book is to introduce you to a variety of strategies that may be used to assist you in differentiating curriculum and instruction in your own classroom. We make the assumption that you have a good working knowledge of the differentiation mindset. If you don't, we would encourage you to read Carol Tomlinson's (1999, 2001, 2003) work for a complete discussion of the topic.

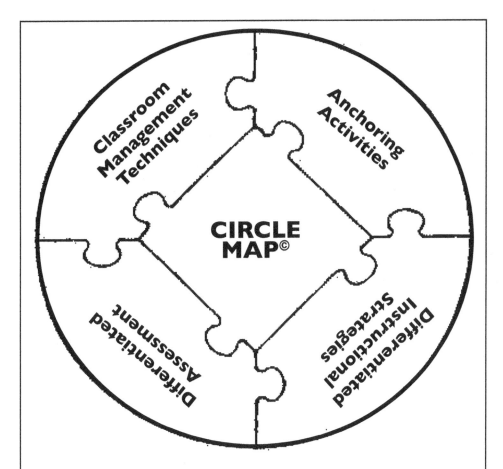

Figure 1. Creating an Integrated Response for Challenging Learners Equitably: A Model by Adams and Pierce©.

CHAPTER 2

EXIT CARDS

Overview

An exit card is a tool used by teachers to gather data about student learning. Generally, exit cards are used to gather formative data that a teacher can then use to plan the next step. The exit card is provided to students at the end of a lesson and the teacher collects the cards as students either exit the classroom or exit one activity before going on to the next in the same classroom. Exit cards also may be known by other names, such as ticket to leave or door pass. Exit cards generally only have a few questions for students to answer. Sometimes the card may ask students to respond to an overall idea that was discussed in class; at other times students may have two or three math problems to work on that are similar to problems demonstrated in class.

How and When to Use Exit Cards

Exit cards are used at the end of a class, an activity, or a lesson. The teacher collects the completed exit cards and sorts the cards into piles based on the students' responses. There may be a group of students who clearly understand the ideas presented in the lesson and another group of students who clearly have gaps in their knowledge. There may be other students who fall between the two groups. The information from the exit cards allows the teacher to plan the next steps of instruction to address the different learning needs of the students.

 DOI: 10.4324/9781003234647-2

Directions for Making Exit Cards

Exit cards are simple to design. For example, an exit card can be a piece of paper that the student uses to write down answers to a set of questions dictated by the teacher. Students may use their own paper or the teacher may hand out paper from the classroom recycle box. Index cards and Post-It® Notes also are simple and easy to use as exit cards, although somewhat more expensive. Some teachers may wish to customize their exit cards for a specific lesson or activity.

How This Strategy Fits in the CIRCLE MAP

Exit cards are an important data-gathering tool for formative assessment in the differentiated classroom. As such, they are essential to the "differentiated assessment" component of the CIRCLE MAP.

Examples

The examples we have chosen include exit cards that can be readily adapted to many topics. These cards were created by real teachers who used them in their own classrooms. When possible, we have included the comments from the teachers and their colleagues with the intention that the comments may provide additional insight to using the exit card for another topic.

For example, Susan Flowers is a middle school language arts teacher who has decided to implement exit cards in her class this year. She creates a card to help her determine who understands how to diagram a compound sentence. She designs a card that includes three sentences that will establish whether or not students understand how to diagram compound sentences. As she collects the cards, Susan can easily determine who has complete, partial, or little understanding. This will allow her to determine the entry point for each student in the next lesson.

Template

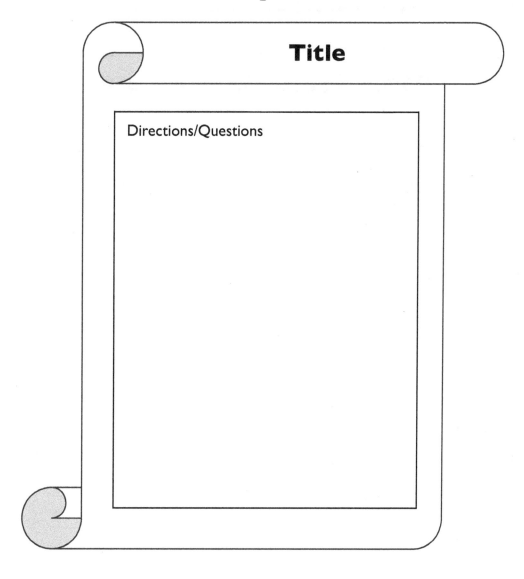

Title

Directions/Questions

Name:_____ Date:_____

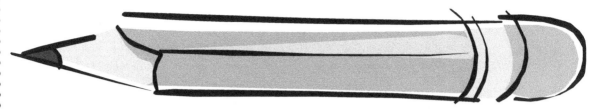

Paper Progress Exit Card

Keep in mind the due date of your paper: _____

1. How is your paper coming?

   _____

   _____

   _____

2. Where do you need to concentrate your effort?

   _____

   _____

   _____

3. Is there anything that I can do to help you get back or stay on track?

   _____

   _____

   _____

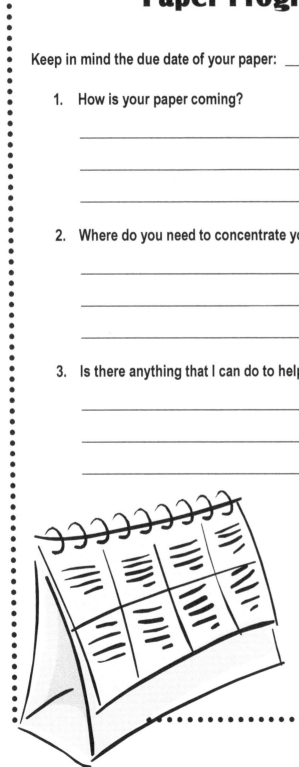

Created by Laura Alexander

Real Teacher Comments

I am currently teaching two sections of advanced eighth-grade writing. The way that the class is set up is that we meet in the computer lab every day. I created a website where I have the daily agenda and all of the materials available. For the most part, the students work through the materials at their own pace, but I am there to provide help, to explain things differently if needed, and of course, to make sure that the students are on task. Usually in the course of the 46-minute period, they have a quick write, a minilesson that normally consists of something grammatical or relates to the type of paper they are working on. The rest of the time is spent on a larger writing assignment, which they typically have 4–5 weeks to complete.

This exit card comes about halfway through their paper, so I use it to monitor where they are and to have them reflect on their progress. I used the card for two different sections of my advanced writing classes. It was actually most interesting to compare the results of the two classes.

My first-period class is a really hard-working group of kids, and they gave some very honest feedback. I didn't have a single person answer that he or she wanted me to do anything additional to help. Even if they admitted that they were behind, they stepped up to take the responsibility for themselves, which made me proud of them.

My fifth-period group, however, was a different story. They have class right before lunch, and overall, they are a very talkative group. They had just earned themselves a new seating chart because of excessive talking and not doing their work, so as a whole, they were not very happy with me, and that showed in their responses. Even though they had been doing the same work as the other class, there was a constant theme of complaining about too much work, and quite a few students even admitted to not having started their papers yet. I was disappointed that this group had been a little more immature and showed that they needed to step up to realize that they must take responsibility.

Overall, I think that it was really helpful to me to quickly get an overview of where everyone was. I check in with them on a regular basis, but I think some of them felt like this was a different method of communicating with me, which they appreciated.

—Laura Alexander (Teacher)

I like your use of the exit cards for progress monitoring. Sometimes I do something similar as a bell-work question ("How much more time do you need for your project?"), but it makes so much more sense to ask that question at the end of class so I can use the students' responses to plan for the next day. I'm curious whether more students ask questions about the assignment using the exit card than would ordinarily in class. I've found that when it comes to clarifying assignments, a lot of my accelerated students are reluctant to ask questions in front of the whole group for fear of embarrassment or appearing as though they weren't paying attention. The exit card might be more comfortable for some.

—Lisa (Colleague)

I noticed that your card is used as a progress report. This is a good use of the card and should help you in aiding the students with their reports.

—Kim (Colleague)

I think an exit card is a wonderful way to monitor student progress in writing. My students have a very large comprehensive research project at the end of the year. This includes a research paper, a speech, a display board, and a costume. I am constantly trying to keep track of where each student is in the process. I will try to use this. Hopefully it will save me some headaches!

—Jennifer (Colleague)

Name:_____ Date:_____

Punctuation Exit Card
English 8 Honors

Directions: Today we reviewed the correct use of punctuation with appositives and compound sentences. We also worked on revising our autobiography drafts.

Considering this . . .

1. What are two important rules to remember when using commas?

   _____

   _____

   _____

2. List one question you want answered concerning our work with punctuation or your draft.

   _____

   _____

   _____

3. What do you think you know well, or what do you feel you have confidently mastered?

   _____

   _____

   _____

Created by Ami Brown

Real Teacher Comments

This exit card was made for my eighth-grade English honors class. I am sure it appears pretty basic, but this is their first big assignment. This is also our first year for block scheduling, so that has demanded some adjustments as well. We are covering simple grammar usage (e.g., punctuation, errors) and vocabulary, and they have been working on a "Phase Autobiography."

This card was meant to judge the students' perception of what they feel is important, and also what they feel they have mastered. Sometimes what we think as teachers doesn't always match up with the students' reactions. I hope to utilize exit cards in the near future as we begin to work with our literature. I think this would work really well as we explore thematic issues, symbolism, and so on in the material we read.

—Ami Brown (Teacher)

Pay It Forward

Today we watched the film *Pay It Forward*. Complete this exit card to show your understanding of the film.

What is the main idea that the writer of this film wanted to share?

_____

_____

_____

How can you apply Trevor's principle to your life?

_____

_____

_____

Why do you think the writer ended the story as he did?

_____

_____

_____

Tell at least two ways Trevor's idea changed the lives of others.

_____

_____

_____

Created by Susan Burson

Real Teacher Comments

This exit card was made for my English honors class for our study of the overarching idea of altruism. Although the use of film in addition to literature usually keeps students engaged, I wanted to make sure that students could determine the main idea, figure out a way to apply the principle to their life, and generate ideas about the author's purpose.

Most students could determine the main purpose, some had difficulty applying the principle to their own lives, and most did not understand why the author chose to end the story in the manner he did.

—Susan Burson (Teacher)

I like the idea of using a film to demonstrate a major concept that is also found in the literature that students are reading. I know my class would definite enjoy an appropriate movie every once in a while. But the exit card is a great way to ensure that students paid attention and benefited from the experience.

—Kim (Colleague)

3-2-1 Summarizer

Name **three** types of details that can be added to increase the length and the quality of your rough draft:

_____   _____   _____

Add **two** details to improve this sentence: The meal was good.

_____

_____

What is **one** question you have about what we have learned today?

_____

Created by Karrie Hamilton

Real Teacher Comments

As a literacy coach, I have been working with our seventh grade in using the 6 + 1 Trait® Writing model. This week's lesson was on revision, specifically adding details. I shared five types of details that can be added to make a piece of writing longer, more specific, and more interesting:

1. Number Details: Age, weight, date, length, width, time, elapsed time, score, price, and so on.
2. Name Details: Replace pronouns (e.g., he, she, it, they) with the specific names of people, places, and things.
3. Sensory Details: Use the senses to describe how something looks, sounds, tastes, feels, and smells.
4. Comparison Details: Use simile, metaphor, personification, and analogy to describe.
5. "Snapple Facts": Use interesting and surprising facts rather than boring information that people already know. (I gave students a list of "Snapple Facts" from the Snapple website as an example of interesting facts.)

Students selected a rough draft they had already written to revise by adding different types of details described in the lesson. This exit card was the culminating activity for each class period. I used this activity in all five seventh-grade writing classes, including the high-ability/honors class. By the end of the first class, I already knew that the exit card needed to be revised. Some students didn't have a question about the lesson, so I let them give a comment instead about how this activity made their writing better.

The exit card worked great with students. They liked filling it out, and it gave me all of the information I needed to measure the success of the lesson. I think students liked being able to recap what they had learned and show what they knew. The fact that it was their ticket out the door was also a motivator. I found that some of the kids who I had thought understood really didn't. They listed three adjectives instead of three types of details. This is a strategy I will definitely use with students in the future. I think a similar activity would work great as a preassessment for my high-ability classes.

—Karrie Hamilton (Teacher)

I am so excited about the way you are using your exit card for writing instruction! I definitely will start thinking about how this can be used in my class. I also like how you adjusted the feedback to meet your students' needs. It's amazing how these simple exit cards can open our eyes to exactly what our students know or don't know and ways to communicate this with them. I will certainly use these again to inform my instruction!

—Andrea (Colleague)

I also appreciate how you mention that a similar activity could work as a quick preassessment!

—Ruth (Colleague)

"Ticket to get out the door" is definitely the incentive middle schoolers need to actually write something sometimes. I love that these can easily be scanned, so students can't leave unless they have put some effort into answering the questions or making a comment.

—Ellen (Colleague)

As I was thinking about exit cards, I thought I might like to try adding a pre-assessment question to mine. I think I could quickly assess today's idea right along with preassessing the next day's topic. It would help focus my lesson delivery, even after the planning had taken place.

—Robynn (Colleague)

Plot Exit Card

1. What is one event that occurs in the rising action of the story?

   _____

   _____

   _____

2. What event occurs at the climax of the story?

   _____

   _____

   _____

3. What is one event that occurs in the falling action of the story?

   _____

   _____

   _____

Created by Suzanne Jones

Real Teacher Comments

I used this exit card to assess my students' abilities to apply their knowledge of the story plot line diagram to an actual story. I easily found which kids in each class were still having trouble identifying the climax of a story. I went over the plot line for the story in a small group with those students still needing more practice. We discussed several more stories they were all familiar with and discussed the plot lines for these stories. I did this while the other students were reading silently. I felt that those students I worked with found the small-group work beneficial.

—Suzanne Jones (Teacher)

This is a hard concept for students. Using stories they are familiar with will help them see the action more easily.

—Loretta (Colleague)

Reading Preferences Exit Card

1. Think about past experiences with novels taught in class. Do you prefer independent reading and work, small-group reading circles, or teacher-led reading and discussion?

   _____

   _____

2. Would you rather read fiction or nonfiction? _____

3. Please explain in two sentences your answers for 1 and 2.

   _____

   _____

   _____

   _____

Created by Stephen Merkle

Real Teacher Comments

I am planning a novel unit for my 10th-grade honors classes to begin in the next couple of weeks. I like to mix up how the novel is addressed, and this time I am giving the students some choice. So far, their varied responses have shown a bit of honesty. Some prefer teacher-led discussions because they admit that sometimes they don't "get" what the author means. Some want the chance to work at their own pace because they like the solitude. Others want the chance to read and discuss with their peers. I tried this last year, and I had a lot of success with the reading circle strategy. They also dabbled with reading journal formats (sticky notes, "Dear diary," and a morphed-Cornell method). My group thought it was funny that they had to give me a pass to leave at the bell.

—Stephen Merkle (Teacher)

This is a great idea to find out what your students prefer. They probably think you are slightly off with requiring a pass to get out of class. Glad you were able to make it fun and useful.

—Julie (Colleague)

Aren't exit cards a helpful strategy for teachers? We're able to gain some valuable input from our students, which can drive our future lesson planning. I'm sure the responses to your questions will let you know how to approach your upcoming novel study.

—Gail (Colleague)

Looking for America

Pretend you experienced the events the author wrote about in the story you just read. Write a postcard to a friend back home explaining why you now feel helpless after visiting with the McNeelys.

Elizabeth Partridge
San Francisco, California
USA

Created by Jessica Rogers

Real Teacher Comments

My sixth-grade language arts students just read a story about segregation in the South in the 1960s. I wanted to assess whether my students understood the main concept of this story: segregation and how it affected the character. After collecting the exit cards, I ended up with two piles: students who understood the concept and students for whom the concept was not clear. Luckily, the pile of cards from students who understood was much larger! This was such an easy way to assess my students' understanding of the story. I will definitely use exit cards in the future.

—Jessica Rogers (Teacher)

I liked your idea of using a postcard as the exit card. Hopefully the students will be able to make their learning a little more meaningful. I also like the ease of the sorting technique to find out who knows [the material] and who doesn't.

—Alicia (Colleague)

Don't you just love the quick assessment? If need be, you could run through the skill again with those who didn't quite get it. I am totally sold on exit cards and have shared them with other teachers. They were interested as well.

—Debra (Colleague)

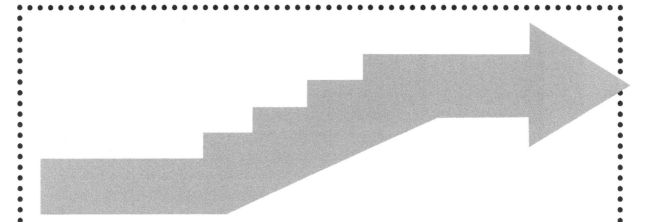

Instruction Manual Exit Card

1. *Write a sentence in passive voice, and then rewrite the sentence in active voice.*

   PV: _____

   _____

   AV: _____

   _____

2. *What is one way to make instructions clearer?*

   _____

   _____

3. *What questions do you have about the instruction manual project?*

   _____

   _____

Created by Lisa Sarjeant

Real Teacher Comments

I used my exit card on the introductory day for a mini-unit on giving effective instructions (eighth-grade accelerated language arts). We looked at some funny, bad directions I found online and talked about ways to improve them. We discussed active and passive voice and why active voice makes for better directions. Finally, we looked at project requirements and brainstormed project ideas (students will be writing a set of instructions for their parents to use a technological device, students' choice).

The results of the exit card questions were very helpful. Only three or four students didn't grasp active versus passive voice, so the next day in class, I was able to pull those few aside and go over the concept with them again. That saved me the time of reteaching a lesson to the whole group, and saved most of the students the boredom of hearing about a concept they already knew.

On Question 2, all students provided a solid example of how to improve a set of directions, so I knew that I could move on from there. Question 3 was very interesting; nearly every student asked a question about the project, including several students who rarely speak in front of the whole group. At the beginning of the next class period, I shuffled the cards and read each question, answered it, and then moved on without identifying the student. I think the exit cards provided a safer means of asking questions for those kids. It was effective!

—Lisa Sarjeant (Teacher)

I also like the type of question students can use to express their feelings about the class and their particular needs. I have many shy students in each of my classes, and this gives them an opportunity to share something without being identified to the class. I frequently ask students to do quick-writes on sticky notes or scrap paper, and then I read them aloud without names. This cuts down on duplicate answers and everyone is engaged in learning at the same time.

—Jeri (Colleague)

I would have asked a lot more questions in eighth grade had my teacher used an exit card like this. The combination of shyness and my attempts to be cool did not lead to much exploratory questioning! Keeping it anonymous gives those shy students another opportunity to gain understanding.

—Jason (Colleague)

Reading Analysis Exit Card

Even though *The Boy in the Striped Pajamas* is told by an outside, third-person narrator, it **seems** more like it is being told by Bruno because . . .

_____

_____

_____

_____

_____

_____

_____

_____

_____

_____

_____

_____

_____

_____

_____

_____

_____

_____

_____

Created by Tracy Schwerin

Real Teacher Comments

For my sixth-grade language arts class, I took a concept that a few kids had mentioned (but we have not yet studied) and I created an exit card to sample everyone's thoughts.

My students know the difference between first-person and third-person narration, but we have not yet studied the different between third-person limited and third-person omniscient. Some students had mentioned how it really seems like Bruno is the narrator in *The Boy in the Striped Pajamas* even though he doesn't say "I" to the reader. My exit card had them explain why it seems like Bruno is the narrator.

Many students wrote that most of the book's details are about Bruno. The best student answer was, "The narrator tells everything Bruno is thinking," an almost perfect definition of an omniscient third-person point of view. Another great answer was, "It seems like the things are going through a 9-year-old's mind."

I'm glad I used this card because I now have some great, simple definitions to share with the class.

—Tracy Schwerin (Teacher)

The open-ended response was a good choice for an exit slip. Asking students to explain will give you more in-depth information.

—April (Colleague)

Work Preferences
Exit Card

1. Do you think today's assignment was too easy, too hard, or just right? Why?

   _____

   _____

   _____

   _____

2. Do you like checking your own answers with another student, or do you prefer the traditional method of teachers telling you the answers while you check your own work? Why or why not?

   _____

   _____

   _____

   _____

Created by Teri Vasquez

Real Teacher Comments

This was used for a seventh-grade language arts class. I needed feedback about the difficulty level of a lesson I had just taught. I am trying to make my lessons moderately challenging and meaningful for my students. I also wanted their opinions about their comfort level with two ways of checking answers for a future activity. This exit card provided answers to both of my questions and allowed me to plan more effective lessons.

—Teri Vasquez (Teacher)

CHAPTER 3

CHOICE BOARDS

Overview

A choice board, sometimes called a Tic-Tac-Toe board, is a tool to provide students with choice and challenge. It has nine squares in a three by three array. Directions are placed in each square. Students choose three squares to complete to make a winning tic-tac-toe: three in a row, three in a column, or three diagonally. The directions may be for a product or for extended practice. Choices can provide enrichment, acceleration, or additional practice, depending on how the choice board is designed. Generally, students are producing three products, which would provide formative or summative data for the teacher.

How and When to Use Choice Boards

Choice boards can be used at the beginning or end of a unit or anywhere in between. The length of time students have to complete their three choices varies with the teacher's purpose. Some choice boards are designed to be completed in a week (e.g., one that deals with weekly spelling words). Other times, a choice board may last for longer periods of time, depending on the complexity of the choices or the length of time the teacher chooses for activities to be completed. Choice boards may be tiered to accommodate varying learning needs when a wider range of choices and challenge is needed. The completed activities from the choice board can be used by the teacher to plan the next steps of instruction, to assess students' progress or level of understanding, or as a means of assigning grades.

 DOI: 10.4324/9781003234647-3

Directions for Making Choice Boards

Choice boards are simple to design using the template provided here. The table function in a word processing program is another easy way to create choice boards. Each cell contains directions for or a description of an activity to be completed. Once the activities are appropriately sequenced to allow for variety no matter how the student chooses to make tic-tac-toe, the choice board can then be printed and copied. We have found that putting the activities on Post-It® Notes allows for experimentation with multiple arrangements until the "best" placement is found. Then we use a word processing program to produce the final form of the choice board for students. Choose the way that works best with your particular style of creating classroom materials. Keep in mind that some activities will require rubrics while others may be self-checking and students will need to know where to find answer keys.

How This Strategy Fits in the CIRCLE MAP

Choice boards fit in the "differentiated instructional strategies" component of the CIRCLE MAP. They provide a simple yet lively means to vary the process or product in a differentiated classroom.

Examples

The examples we have chosen to include here address specific topics. These choice boards were created by real teachers who used them in their own classrooms. When possible, we have included the comments from the teachers and their colleagues with the intention that the comments may provide additional insight to creating your own choice board. We have tried to include a wide variety of topics to give you a number of ideas for making your own.

For example, in Zach Carter's advanced English class, students are busily working on a choice board he has designed as part of his unit on *Great Expectations*. In each of the nine blocks, he has placed an interesting activity to reinforce or enrich the concepts he has chosen. Zach has been careful to include activities that will appeal to various strengths and learning profiles. He has developed some activities that encourage written responses and some that are more analytic. Some activities require research, and some rely on reinforcing facts. By providing activities at a variety of readiness levels as well as addressing different learning profiles, he is ensuring that his students will find challenging and meaningful activities to complete.

Template
Title of Choice Board

Directions: Please select three assignments to complete for a winning tic-tac-toe (3 in the same row, 3 in the same column, or 3 diagonally).

Conflict Activity

English 8 Honors

Directions: Each of the selections we have read deals with conflict in some manner. In order to show your understanding of this literary element, choose three activities from the Choice Board. Remember—your three choices must make a horizontal or diagonal line.

What Do You Know?	Let's Be Creative!	Apply It!
Define Conflict. On your paper, offer your own definition of conflict. This definition should include: • an explanation of what conflict is (internal and external), and • one example of conflict from the stories we have read.	**Show It!** Draw an illustration that reflects conflict from one of the selections we have read. Your illustration should contain: • the characters involved, • an accurate/appropriate illustration, and • a caption that sums up the illustration.	**How Can We Help?** Write a letter of advice to one of the characters who was involved in a conflict of some manner. Your letter should include: • a proper heading and closing, • an accurate description of the conflict, and • advice on how this conflict can be fixed.
Create a Conflict Chart. Complete a chart that shows the various types of conflict and how each one is or is not resolved in the stories we have read. Your chart must contain examples of both internal and external conflict(s).	**Write Your Own Ending!** Think about a conflict from one of the selections we have read that is **not** resolved. How would you fix it? Your ending should contain: • at least three paragraphs of original writing, and • an accurate/believable resolution for a conflict that was left unresolved.	**Display It!** Create a billboard that displays conflict. The billboard should include: • a conflict that is apparent from our readings, • an explanation as to why it is a conflict, and • a motto that advertises why this conflict should be avoided.
Complete a Concept Map. Complete a concept map for the term "conflict." The map should contain: • conflict and its definition as a center point, and • at least four branches that contain examples of conflict from our readings.	**Create a Cover.** Create a CD cover/jacket for one of the selections we have read. Your CD cover should contain: • an appropriate illustration/title, and • the names of at least four songs that would represent the conflict(s) in our selections.	**Make Rules to Remember.** Using the information from our readings, create a list of conflict rules for our characters to follow. Your list should contain: • at least five rules, and • a brief explanation of why these would be good rules for our characters to follow.

Created by Ami Brown

Real Teacher Comments

I used this choice board with my English 8 honors class. We have started a unit in our literature book, and many of the selections we are reading deal with relationships in some way. The literary term that is the focus for this unit is "conflict," both internal and external. I always like to have my students do something creative with their readings, and this was a good opportunity to put my ideas to work.

The students liked the format. I usually just give my students a list of possible reaction projects, and the choice board seems to make the purpose of their work more obvious. My students were more aware of what type of activity (basic comprehension vs. creative application) they were doing. I will definitely use this idea with my other units throughout the year.

—Ami Brown (Teacher)

Name:_____ Date:_____

Tic-Tac-Toe Board: Canterbury Tales

Directions: After completing your reading of the *Canterbury Tales* outlined in the syllabus, complete three of the activities below.

Create **trading cards** for each of the pilgrims described in the Prologue. For each character, include a picture, as well as the character's occupation (with an explanation), ranking in the feudal system, personal vices, and personal motto (to be created by you).	Research the shrine of Saint Thomas a' Becket, whom all the pilgrims were travelling to see. Create a **PowerPoint presentation** of no fewer than 10 slides detailing your findings.	Write a **manual** for the Knight in the "Wife's Tale" describing what the modern woman wants. Include sections on how men should treat women, how women should treat each other, family dynamics, and career goals.
Write a **modernization** of one of the tales we read in *Canterbury Tales*. Update the setting, characters, and situation, but stay true to the overarching idea (message) of the story.	Make a **board game** centered around the *Canterbury Tales*. This game should serve as a review of all of the tales we read, in addition to the life of Chaucer. The design of your game board and pieces should mirror the time period.	Research the feudal system that plays such a big role in Chaucer's book. Create a **poster** illustrating the hierarchy, along with a one-page paper that explains your poster.
Research the trip that the pilgrims would have taken on their way to Canterbury. Make a **map** outlining their journey and create a **travel brochure** written for people of their day advertising the pilgrimage to St. Thomas's shrine.	Create your own **graphic novel** version of one of Chaucer's tales. You may do the drawings yourself, or use the computer and clip art to tell the tale. Your finished version should be presented in book form.	Write your own **frame story**, à la Chaucer. You may write about any topic of your choice, but it must illustrate your understanding of the frame story, and like both Chaucer's and Boccaccio's characters, your characters must also be a group traveling together.

This paper will be turned in with your projects. Please complete the following steps before turning in your final draft.

1. Name: _____ Period: _____
2. Please mark your choices on the board above.
3. Please turn this sheet in with your projects by: _____

Created by Jenny Duguid

Real Teacher Comments

I did this choice board for my junior and senior Literary Movement classes. We are just finishing up *Canterbury Tales*, and I am using this project as their final grade. At first, some of my students were a little overwhelmed with the number of choices; but after we talked through each option, they began to get excited. I let them have some time in class to work, but a lot of this they will be doing at home as well. I'm excited to see the end results. I tried to make sure that each tic-tac-toe involved a variety of activities (writing, research, and creating something). I think my students appreciated the breadth of choices.
—Jenny Duguid (Teacher)

Wow! If I were a student in your class, I would be so excited! I can see how it would be overwhelming, but I bet they are going to love the freedom. The creativity and various intelligences [the activity] reaches look great! I also think it does a good job validating what they were expected to learn.
—Trisha (Colleague)

Your *Canterbury Tales* tic-tac-toe is awesome. You did an incredible job. I'm sure your students appreciated the options you offered to them.
—Susan (Colleague)

When I read your title, I thought there was no way your board would apply to my students. But I love it! I think it could easily be adapted to another grade.
—Allison (Colleague)

Snapshot Tic-Tac-Toe

Select three options from the board below to make a tic-tac-toe.

Rewrite a portion of a fairy tale, turning the climax into a snapshot.	Choose a picture or process of nature and create a snapshot that can be used to educate the public about the topic.	Write a snapshot about a sporting event. Pretend you are the commentator!
Pretend you are a police officer or a crime scene investigator. Write a snapshot of the crime or crime scene you are investigating.	Get together with at least one other person. You are the "sight" person. Your partner(s) is/are responsible for one of the other five senses. Work together to create a snapshot!	Choose a picture from the pile your teacher provides. Use the image to write a snapshot.
Choose a song and express its contents via a snapshot.	Write and perform a play in which you are able to convey all of the information from a snapshot.	Write a snapshot that gives detailed instructions for completing a task.

Created by Amanda Fisher

Real Teacher Comments

This is a copy of the choice board I am doing as a culmination of my snapshot unit. The kids have really been responding well so far. They like the fact that it addresses multiple intelligences and that there are a wide variety of choices. Several of them have mentioned that they like being able to think more abstractly. Prior to this assignment, they had to write about a "real-life" event—something they had actually experienced. I really look forward to seeing what they produce.

—Amanda Fisher (Teacher)

Name:_____ Date:_____

Tic-Tac-Toe Board

Objective: Make a tic-tac-toe by choosing and completing three activities from the table below. Cross out the square once you have completed each revision strategy.

Word Choice	**Organization**	**Word Choice**
Add five "name details" to your piece (name your nouns: people, places, and/or things).	Add a "hook" to your introduction that draws in your reader (e.g., a question, an interesting fact).	Replace four "dead verbs" with action verbs (e.g., replace "get" with "purchased," replace "went" with "trudged").
Word Choice	**Voice**	**Word Choice**
Change four different "shades of a word" (e.g., instead of "red," use "crimson," instead of "hot" use "sizzling").	Add one example of figurative language to your piece (e.g., simile, metaphor, personification, analogy).	Add three "number details" to your piece (e.g., dates, ages, temperatures, lengths, weights, scores, prices, times).
Ideas	**Word Choice**	**Organization**
Use the revising questions to mark your rough draft: 1. What is the best part? (Mark with an *) 2. Where could you add more detail? (Mark with a +) 3. What is confusing? (Mark with a ?) 4. What could be cut? (Mark with a –)	Add three sensory details to your piece—describe using your senses how something looks, sounds, tastes, smells, and feels.	Add three transition sentences to your piece using words and phrases like "the next day," "an hour later," "finally," and "however."

Created by Karrie Hamilton

Real Teacher Comments

I developed my choice board to use with one of the seventh-grade classes with which I have been working on revision in writing. We have been learning about and using the 6 + 1 Trait® Writing all year, and now we are focusing on revising existing pieces of writing. My board contains nine revision strategies that we have already studied at some point this year. I labeled the board according to which trait each strategy addressed. The students liked the choice board technique for revising. They liked that they didn't have to complete all of the tasks, although some students did attempt to make all nine revisions. Others asked if they could apply the choices to a second piece of writing once they had completed their initial tic-tac-toe, and others asked about making two tic-tac-toes within one piece.

—Karrie Hamilton (Teacher)

We teach the writing process using the 6 + 1 traits, also. Revising and editing are tough for most students! I think this will make it more fun and interesting. Thanks for sharing!

—Kerri (Colleague)

Name:_____   Date:_____

"The Mad Moon"
by Stanley G. Weinbaum

Select three options from the board below to make a tic-tac-toe.

Which creature or character is your favorite? Why?	**You are the author of the story—what would you change? Why?**	**Grant and Lee get married and live on Io. Describe what their life might be like.**
What invention would you create to make Grant's life easier on Io? Describe it.	**What new plants could be discovered on Io, and what could their uses be?**	**What new creatures could be discovered on Io? How would they be adapted to live in their environment?**
Create a poster to advertise the story so people will want to read it.	**Decide which character you'd like to spend the day with. Write two paragraphs explaining why you chose this character and what you would do.**	**Make a comic strip of the main events in this story. You must have at least six squares. Each square must have a caption.**

Created by Suzanne Jones

Real Teacher Comments

I created this tic-tac-toe board to accompany the science fiction story "The Mad Moon." The story's setting is on one of the moons of Jupiter. It is very difficult for sixth-grade kids to read because of the vocabulary and the imaginary setting. We had to keep track of the different creatures and plants encountered. The tic-tac-toe board was a success. The kids really enjoyed choosing what activities they'd like to do. It was a fun final product choice for the story. Some kids wanted to do all of the squares. I was very pleased with how the kids responded.

—Suzanne Jones (Teacher)

These look like activities children would like to do. It speaks well for the board that some students wanted to do all of the squares. It makes you want to do more!

—Loretta (Colleague)

How creative! Way to go! Sometimes it's so difficult to get concepts like that across.

—Debra (Colleague)

CHOICE BOARD – ENGLISH 10
POETRY AND POETIC ELEMENTS

Pick one of the three rows (across). Then read the poems and ancillary content, analyze the poems and content using the key elements, and complete the activity for that row. Consult the corresponding rubric for your respective assignment to see how it will be evaluated.

CONTENT	ELEMENTS	ACTIVITY
Read Robert Frost's "Stopping by Woods on a Snowy Evening" and "After Apple-Picking." Use a T-chart to record observations of symbols in each poem.	Symbolic meaning, word connotations and associations, sensory imagery	Prepare an oral interpretation of the poems. This "spoken-word" tribute should provide insight into the symbolism from the poems and incorporate a unique perspective to similar images addressed in the poems.
Read Carl Sandburg's "Jazz Fantasia," then listen to the "Charlie Parker" station on Pandora (free Internet radio).	Sound effects, onomatopoeia, speaker's slang, musical imagery	Create a reflective piece of art that represents the style of music Sandburg describes. Artwork should embody the jazz style and include a brief summary explaining motivations and decisions.
Read "The Legend" by Garrett Hongo and run an Internet search for information on Rene Descartes's *Cogito, ergo sum.*	Imagery, free verse, poetic tone, interpretation of beliefs	Write a 300–400 word essay evaluating Hongo's use of poetic elements to present a philosophy of life in the poem. Consider the elements and the research you find as you analyze the poem.

Created by Stephen Merkle

Name:_____ Date:_____

RUBRICS FOR POEM ACTIVITIES

I. *Oral Interpretation:*

Symbolism evaluated   _____/10

Original insight   _____/10

Performance in class   _____/10

Inclusion of poetic elements   _____/10

Use of vocabulary   _____/10

TOTAL _____/50

II. *Jazz Artwork:*

Product dimensions (24" x 30")   _____/10

Effective use of art medium   _____/10

Artistic originality   _____/10

Written summary   _____/10

Style and imagery   _____/10

TOTAL _____/50

III. *Essay Evaluation:*

Interpretation of poem   _____/10

Philosophy of author   _____/10

Inclusion of research   _____/10

Writing style and tone   _____/10

Organization of thoughts   _____/10

TOTAL _____/50

Teacher Comments and Suggestions: _____

_____

_____

_____

_____

Real Teacher Comments

I created this choice board for my poetry unit. I have used choice boards in the past when I taught seventh-grade English. From my observations, students always seem receptive to choice as long as they identify or connect with something. Reflecting on differentiation, the "readiness/interest/learning style/affect" section was my inspiration for the choice board creation. Students either like or hate poetry, it seems. I decided to make the activities focus on nontraditional poetry assessments because of that attitude.

—Stephen Merkle (Teacher)

I like the organization and categorization of your choice board. It really helps me to visualize the steps a student would take in selecting an activity.

—Melinda (Colleague)

This is a good example of differentiation. I like how you allowed the students to represent their work in three ways (oral, visual art, or written).

—Marlon (Colleague)

Choice Board

Complete a winning tic-tac-toe horizontally or diagonally.

Text Features	Vocabulary	Skimming and Scanning
Create a new title for "Messaging Mania." Explain why you chose the new title and how it tells about the article.	Using the vocabulary words from "Messaging Mania," write a paragraph that includes at least four of the seven words.	Read an article in your literature book. Develop five questions a person could answer from scanning the article. Have a friend scan the article to answer your questions.
Name the titles of three books, articles, or magazines you have read. Explain how the titles helped you understand the information.	Find five multiple meaning words. Draw a word web showing the definitions.	Choose an article from your literature book. Skim the article to find out what it is about. Write down the important information you found while skimming.
Write a paragraph about a text feature you have found helpful. Tell how it helped you understand what you were reading.	Draw a picture dictionary of each of the seven vocabulary words from "Messaging Mania."	Scan the article "Ballpark Food." Does it portray ballparks in a positive or negative way? Explain your thoughts.

Created by Jessica Rogers

Real Teacher Comments

I used the choice board to assess three areas my students were working on while reading a story in language arts. Students had to choose from an activity relating to a text feature, vocabulary, and the skill we were currently studying. Of course it created difficulty for students to follow directions when they were told they had to choose one activity from each column. I had the question, "What is a column?" among others that I was not expecting. However, after students began working, they were able to complete each activity. When grading the projects, however, I was not happy about the quality of students' work. Next time I use a choice board, I will definitely discuss the importance of the quality of their work.

—Jessica Rogers (Teacher)

I like the different types of activities that the students have to choose from. I know that there were many choices that would have been of interest to me when I was that age. Would you let your kids do more than three if they completed the required ones?

—Alicia (Colleague)

Good variety of activities. Students will complete better products when you stress the importance of the quality of the work.

—Loretta (Colleague)

Name:_____ Date:_____

Vocabulary Review Choice Board

Directions: This board is for vocabulary review. Select three options from the chart below to make a tic-tac-toe. You may choose only **one** option from each column (you cannot make a vertical tic-tac-toe). **You should use 30 different words total.** All three assignments should be stapled together when completed.

Select 10 vocabulary words and explain how they are related to each other. They may be synonyms, antonyms, different shades of meaning, and so on. Group words together in sets of two, three, or four.	Write a story on any topic using 10 vocabulary words. Circle or underline the vocabulary words in your story.	Find examples of 10 vocabulary words in books, magazines, or online articles. Photocopy or print the pages and circle the vocabulary words. You may also hand-copy the paragraph, but cite your sources!
Write down 10 vocabulary words. For each word, write down a different **form** of the word, and label the new part of speech (e.g., "lumber, v.," "lumber, adj."). Plurals and verb tense changes do not count.	Draw a cartoon strip in which the characters use 10 vocabulary words. Circle or underline the vocabulary words.	Work 10 vocabulary words into your conversations this week. When you do, write down a few lines of the conversation (including the line with the vocabulary word) so that the teacher can see the context in which you used the word.
Write down 10 vocabulary words with identifiable **roots**. For each word, write down two other words that use the same root (these do not have to be vocabulary words).	Create 10 individual vocabulary works of art to illustrate the meanings of 10 words. These may be hand-drawn, cut out of magazines, or printed from the computer.	Use 10 vocabulary words in assignments for other classes this week. Photocopy the pages before you hand them in, and circle the vocabulary word on the photocopy.

Created by Lisa Sarjeant

Real Teacher Comments

My students are accustomed both to working on their own and to having choices in projects and tasks, so they didn't get thrown off too much by the choice board.

This was a vocabulary review week, and I needed an activity for each day anyway (our workbooks don't provide review activities, but I am trying to repeat and reinforce more this year to increase retention), so the choice board fit really nicely into my schedule. We've had more than 200 words at this point in the school year, but I asked them to choose only 30 to complete this assignment.

I also made the "choose only one from each column" stipulation, which was the only thing they raised their hackles about. They argued that it wasn't truly a tic-tac-toe board! Column 1 is knowledge, Column 2 is creative thinking, and Column 3 is application.

Students had 4 days to complete this assignment as homework while we moved forward during class time with another project. Some students became anxious about finishing on time, which I find is pretty typical of this group (and most high-ability students, really), but that did not present a problem at deadline time. I didn't have any late papers. All of the options were chosen by at least one student, with the vocabulary conversation and the comic strip being the most popular.

—Lisa Sarjeant (Teacher)

I love the way you have organized the columns to go from lower order thinking and work skills to higher order thinking and work skills. I have high-ability students all day, every day, so they would love something like this that gets them out of their vocabulary workshop books. Our lists are composed of test prep words that are pertinent to the ACT and the SAT. They would love having this as an alternate option to the humdrum of the workbook!

—Sonny (Colleague)

One of your choices caught my attention. I very much liked the option of using the words in other class assignments. As teachers, we often try to incorporate words from other classes, and some of our students do this. Your choice board provides a great motivator for other students to participate in the carryover.

—Tamra (Colleague)

I really like your choice board selections. This was such a good area to have the students use creative thinking and application. Using a vocabulary list for them to choose and have to utilize the words is a great activity instead of rote memorization! On a side note, I think it's funny that some teenagers tend to argue over small details (e.g., a pseudo tic-tac-toe board) and miss the bigger picture.

—Jennifer (Colleague)

"Rikki-Tikki-Tavi"
Tic-Tac-Toe

Directions: Choose three activities to complete a winning tic-tac-toe to demonstrate your knowledge of Rudyard Kipling's short story "Rikki-Tikki-Tavi."

Research aspects of the mongoose, such as its feeding habits, life cycle, physical characteristics, and so on. Create a mongoose-shaped bookmark and list the facts you discovered on the back.	The confrontation with Nag and Nagaina is Rikki's first experience with his natural enemies. What do the actions of Rikki and the cobras reveal about these three characters?	One example of foreshadowing is when Teddy's father comments about snakes early in the story. Find two or three more examples of foreshadowing. Create a chart or another graphic showing what occurs in each example, when it occurs, and what it foreshadows.
Explain how the battle between Rikki and Karait builds suspense and advances the plot.	In Hindu belief, cobras are serpent kings and queens associated with the god Brahma. Research traditional Hindu tales and compare the cobras in the traditional tales with those in "Rikki-Tikki-Tavi."	What new information does Chuchundra indirectly reveal to Rikki? How does this information advance the plot?
Plot development begins with a description of a basic situation. Describe a basic situation from the story and tell what it reveals about the plot. Along with your explanation, sketch the situation you are describing.	As you read, note conflicts in the story that occur beyond the basic conflict between protagonist and antagonists. They may include: ▪ duty versus fear or self-preservation, ▪ nature versus civilization, ▪ pride versus wisdom, and ▪ love versus vengeance.	Today, mongooses living on islands eat small pets, threaten endangered species, and spread rabies. What steps do you think the governments of these islands should take to solve this problem?

Created by Susan Schweitzer

Real Teacher Comments

Students should have choices as to how they demonstrate understanding and mastery of content and concepts. Constantly assessing students' knowledge through quizzes and tests is unnecessary and becomes mundane for the students as well as for the teachers. With those types of assessments, quite often students learn only what they need for that particular quiz or test. Research tells us that there isn't much carryover to other areas.

Overall, students seemed to enjoy choice boards. Giving students choices as to how they demonstrate their knowledge gives them power. It lets them know that I believe in them. I used this particular choice board for "Rikki-Tikki-Tavi" in both my gifted literature class and my general education literature class. The students in the gifted class completed their choice boards at home while we began a new project in class and had very few questions. They definitely enjoyed being able to choose how they would demonstrate their knowledge of the story.

The majority of the general education students had some questions as we read the story aloud in class, so I incorporated class time for them to work on this. The average and above-average students appeared to enjoy the choice boards and didn't have too much difficulty with their projects. The below-average students found it a bit more challenging and needed much guidance.

—Susan Schweitzer (Teacher)

Name:_____ Date:_____

Tic-Tac-Toe: Reader Response Chart

Directions: Choose three activities on the chart. They may connect vertically or diagonally, but they may **not** connect horizontally.

If you could live in any of the places mentioned in your book, where would it be? Why? Describe the place and what you would do there.	Make a connection between your book and your life. Did a certain character or scene remind you of anything that is important to you? Did a topic or a certain sentence remind you of something that you used to think about?	Discuss believability in your novel. Which events are realistic, and which are not? Do the characters seem like actual human beings, or is it hard to understand why they do the things they do? Does a believable character have a nonhuman quality or make an unrealistic decision?
How does one of the characters change by the end of the book? What evidence does the author give of this change? What do you think causes the change? Is the character likely to go back to the way he or she was? Why or why not?	Discuss the main conflict in your novel and explain how it is resolved.	Compare and contrast yourself with one of the characters in your book. Go beyond physical appearance. Consider questions such as: ■ Do you react the same way in similar situations? ■ Do you relate to people in the same way? ■ Are your lives focused on different issues?
Discuss an important theme in your novel (e.g., forgiveness, making decisions, change, fear). What plot events, conflicts, characters' decisions, and so on helped you identify the theme? Do you think that the theme is relevant (important) to someone your age?	Discuss figurative language in your book. Which types are most frequently used? Give some examples. Are they examples of strong or weak figurative language? Do they add to the writing or just make it seem long? What is their purpose in the book?	Discuss a question raised by the book. What is one question that the book seems to be asking? Does the book give an answer? What would your answer to the question be, or do you still have further questions?

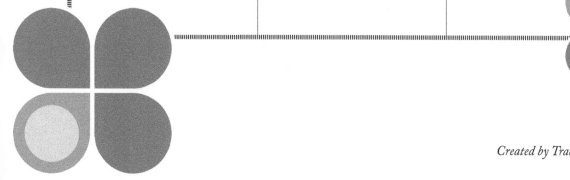

Created by Tracy Schwerin

Real Teacher Comments

I modified an old assignment I used with my class last year for this choice board, and I really like it. The former assignment was a lot more overwhelming (I had them choose seven of the nine prompts), but I found that minimizing the requirement and putting it in a new format made a big difference in how this year's students received it. The answers were a lot more in-depth as well. This board can be used with any book.

—Tracy Schwerin (Teacher)

CHAPTER 4

CUBING

Overview

Cubing is an instructional strategy that has its roots in writing. The strategy uses a cube; on each face of the cube are directions using an action verb (such as create, compare, and analyze) and under each verb is a prompt providing a description of the task. Students roll the cube and complete the activity from the face of the cube that is turned up. They repeat this procedure until they have completed a total of six different tasks. Cubing can be used at any point in a lesson or unit. Like choice boards, cubing is another way to differentiate instruction. Cubing is a novel way to structure a set of activities and to view a topic from multiple angles.

How and When to Use Cubing

Cubing is a versatile strategy that can easily fit into instructional plans at various points—beginning, middle, or end. A cube may be used to introduce a topic and find out what students already know. It may be used in sense-making activities or as a means to determine what students learned from a particular lesson or unit. Students may have their own individual cube or each group may be given a single cube. Cubes can be tiered to accommodate a variety of student cognitive abilities, skill levels, or knowledge of the topic. Sometimes we have heard questions such as, "Couldn't you just list the activities on a sheet of paper and allow students to do the activities in any order?" Although you certainly could do that, we have found that students respond positively when we use strategies that are "fun." As you will see below in the

 DOI: 10.4324/9781003234647-4

teacher comments, students who experienced cubing certainly thought it was a fun and exciting way to learn.

Directions for Making Cubes

Cubes are simple to design using the template provided here. Another alternative and a convenient way to acquire sturdy cubes is to purchase small ($3 \times 3 \times 3$) boxes from a packaging company. Printing the activities on mailing labels and affixing them to the box or template is easier than writing directly on either one. If you choose to write directly on the cube, do so while the cube is unfolded using a fine point, felt tip marker. The table function in a word processing program also can be used to create a cube. Form a 3×4 array, keep the first column intact as well as the middle row, and then delete the extraneous six cells. As another option, you may find it convenient to use The Dice Maker at http://www.toolsforeducators.com. No matter how you form the cube, the format for creating the activity on each face is the same: action verb + prompt.

How This Strategy Fits in the CIRCLE MAP

Cubes fit in the "differentiated instructional strategies" component of the CIRCLE Map. They provide a simple yet lively means to vary the content, process, or product in a differentiated classroom.

Examples

The examples we have chosen address specific topics. These cubes were created by real teachers who used them in their own classrooms. When possible, we have included the comments from the teachers and their colleagues with the intention that the comments may provide additional insight to using the cubes. We have tried to include a wide variety of topics to give you a number of ideas for making your own.

For example, Dawn Miller attended a professional development workshop focusing on a variety of strategies that could be used to differentiate instruction. She particularly liked a strategy called "cubing," but she wondered how her honors English class would respond. She thought they might think using cubes was silly. Her worrying proved unnecessary, because when she introduced the activity, the students were excited! During the activity, each group of three students was assigned a cube. An activity that related to the class's study of *Romeo and Juliet* was written on each face of the cube. Each activity was challenging and required students to use their critical thinking skills. According to the students, it was a great success, and they would like to have the opportunity to work with cubes again.

Template

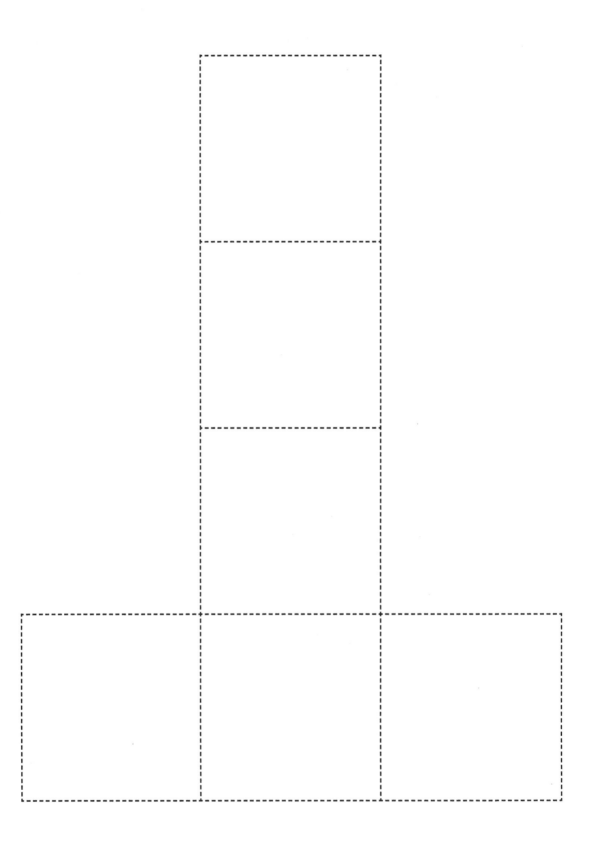

Flowers for Algernon Cube
English 8 Honors

Compare It:
Review Charlie's idea of intelligence and create a Venn diagram in which you compare this with one of our other readings.

Argue for or Against It:
Should all people have the same intelligence? Write at least a two-paragraph response that adequately reflects your ideas.

Define It:
What does intelligence mean? How do we define it? Look up the dictionary definition, and then create a poster that shows your own definition of intelligence.

Analyze It:
In at least three complete paragraphs, explain the message the story makes about the idea of intelligence. Be sure to use examples to support your response.

Associate It:
Compare Charlie's experiences with your own. Have you ever felt different? What does it feel like to be made fun of? Create a drawing that reflects your feelings.

Apply It:
What can we do to help people have a sense of belonging? Create an advice letter that could offer some insight on how to help others gain a sense of belonging.

Real Teacher Comments

My eighth-grade honors class reads *Flowers for Algernon*, and we often take a pretty good look at the idea of intelligence. Many of the activities on my cube are ones that I normally did anyway as separate tasks. My class liked to see all of the different activities together; I think it made them really think about how these activities are all tied to the same theme. Next time I plan to add another "theme" category and then divide the class up into groups according to the different themes.

This would work well with our reading of *The Outsiders*, too. I could have a cube for each theme: growing up, friendship, change, violence, and so on. Oh, the possibilities . . .

—Ami Brown (Teacher)

Character Motivation Cube: *Antony and Cleopatra*
Grades 11 and 12

What **doesn't** the character do that demonstrates what type of person he or she is?

What does the character **do** that demonstrates what type of person he or she is?

What **doesn't** the character say that tells us what type of person he or she is?

What does the character **want?**

What does the character **need?** (Is this different from what the character **thinks** he or she needs?)

What does the character **say** that tells us what type of person he or she is?

Real Teacher Comments

[My juniors and seniors are] about halfway through *Antony and Cleopatra*, and a lot of what we focus on with this play is literary analysis—specifically, how characters' actions and speech illustrate the type of person that they are. This cube has to do with character motivation. My students were excited to get to use the cubes (they are essentially giant elementary students who still fight over stickers), and when they initially saw the questions, they thought that it was going to be really easy. What they didn't realize was that although the questions themselves were fairly simple, the answers were not and required a lot of textual analysis. It really tricked them into digging in their books for proof. I put them in groups and had one person in each group act as the recorder; this led to some great discussion later, and I wanted to make sure that they still had the text references to support what they were saying. When they got a duplicate question, I made them switch characters. Overall, this worked great.

—Jenny Duguid (Teacher)

What I really like about your cube is that it would work with lots of different lessons and stories. I agree—these kids are just big elementary students, and they still love choices and playing and different ways of doing things.

—Kathleen (Colleague)

I agree with Kathleen that this cube could be used for any book. It could also be used for any grade level.

—Lori (Colleague)

Great questions! I could see this being effective in middle school as well. Probably we would want to model it a few times before releasing students into small groups, but definitely a great way for students to analyze characters.

—Mona (Colleague)

I really like that your cube requires deep thought about the text and beyond the text as well. I particularly like how you ask, "What *doesn't* the character do that teaches us about his or her personality?" I often have my students focus on the things the character is saying and doing. I don't often think of the things the characters *aren't* saying or doing. Therefore, my students don't usually think of those things being significant, either. This is a great twist on analyzing characters!

—Laura (Colleague)

What an awesome cubing activity! You really did a great job with the questions you posed. They forced the students to dig deeper and respond with examples from the text. Isn't that what we want students to be able to do? Sometimes we need to rethink how we are going about it, and you did exactly that with your cubing activity and questions. I can't wait to try it with my seventh-grade gifted class.

—Susan (Colleague)

POETRY TERMS CUBE

Write a song to help you remember what the term means.

Create a secret handshake or signal that represents the term.

Write a poem about the term.

Give an example of the term.

Draw a picture that explains the meaning of the term.

Write a mathematical equation for the term (e.g., setting = where + when).

POETRY TERMS CUBE

		Rhythm
	STYLE	
	Rhyme Scheme	
ALLITERATION	Couplet	Tone

Created by Amanda Fisher

Real Teacher Comments

We are currently working on a poetry unit, and a few kids finished early. I gave them these cubes to use to reinforce the terms we've used. They were allowed to work in small groups. Students rolled one cube to find out which of the multiple intelligences they would be using, then rolled the other cube to determine the term they would be using. For example, after rolling their cubes, they may have to write a song to help them remember what a couplet is. They had a lot of fun working, and a few of them said that they really had to think about their answers! One student told me that he understood the terms much better after using the cubes.

—Amanda Fisher (Teacher)

Story Analysis Cube

Draw a picture of the setting in which one of the story's events takes place. How does the setting influence the plot of the story? Next, pick an alternate location for the story and describe how the plot would be different.

Write a letter to your teacher about your reactions to this week's story. What did you like abut it? What did you dislike? How would you improve it?

Draw and illustrate events from the story in a plot diagram format. Identify the exposition, rising action, climax, falling action, and resolution.

Write a descriptive paragraph using all six vocabulary words from this week's story.

Write a paragraph comparing and contrasting your traits to the traits of the main character in this week's story. How are you alike? How are you different?

Identify three literary devices the author uses in this week's story (e.g., simile, alliteration, imagery). Explain how each device helps the reader understand the idea the author is trying to express.

Created by Suzanne Jones

Real Teacher Comments

I created this cube so that I could use it with many different stories that we read this year. The students enjoyed the cube activity overall, but it was difficult for some of them, depending on what they rolled. Picking out literary techniques and their effects and drawing a plot diagram are skills that they are still learning. The kids who rolled those choices weren't thrilled about it. I had them each roll the dice and do whatever they rolled. They didn't like that as well as choosing their own activities on the tic-tac-toe board.

—Suzanne Jones (Teacher)

Nice activities. Do you think that your students would have been more enthusiastic about the assignments that they rolled if they had been more familiar with what you wanted them to complete? It was a good idea to make the cube generic so that you could use it over again with another story.

—Billie (Colleague)

Biography Activities

Created by Rebecca Knight

KNOWLEDGE

Create a list of the 10 things that happened in your famous person's life.

COMPREHENSION

Explain what makes your person famous. What are his or her accomplishments?

APPLICATION

Produce two written entries that could have come from your famous person's personal diary.

ANALYSIS

Create a timeline of important events from your famous person's life.

SYNTHESIS

Produce a movie telling the story of your famous person's life.

EVALUATION

According to the information you have found, what is your famous person's most important accomplishment? Write an essay to support your conclusion.

Real Teacher Comments

We're beginning a unit of biographies, and I wanted to create a cube that could be used with any biography. These activities will help the students gain a better understanding of their famous people by completing activities that cover the whole gamut of Bloom's taxonomy.

—Rebecca Knight (Teacher)

I like the variety this provides. Did you do this activity as a whole class, with one student rolling at a time, or were the kids in partners or small groups? I was also surprised to find how much my eighth graders enjoyed just having something to toss around. It's the simple things.

—Lisa (Colleague)

Cubing Activity for "Why Books Are Dangerous"

Complete the following activities after reading "Why Books Are Dangerous," by Neil Gaiman.

In 1–2 paragraphs, summarize what happens to Neil after he read the book *1001 Jolly Interesting Things a Boy Can Do.*

What can you infer about the climate of Neil's school from his meeting with the headmaster?

Predict what will happen after Neil's book is confiscated by the headmaster.

What is the definition of the word "confiscated"?

Describe two ways the author says books can be dangerous.

In at least two paragraphs, compare one of the events that causes Neil to get in trouble to a time you were in trouble.

Real Teacher Comments

This cube is for students to complete after reading an essay about the author's experience as a young boy who liked to read all kinds of books. The books often caused the boy to get in trouble for various reasons.

This short essay was included in our sixth-grade literature textbook. I thought it was great! The textbook is *Glencoe Reading With Purpose Course I Literature*, and the essay is titled "Why Books Are Dangerous" and was written by Neil Gaiman.

I looked over my students' responses to the cubing activity. Some were fantastic, but most were not. I am not lucky enough to have classes with the majority being high ability. Most of mine are the average and below-average students with a couple of move-ins who, after digging through paperwork, I discovered are high ability. Because the responses required a great deal of writing, as I wanted written responses to literature, students who like to write did excellent work, and those who don't like to write whined the entire time. While the high-ability students were working, I noticed that they were intensely thinking about their answers. When reading their responses, I found that they provided a lot of detail and explained their thought processes. It is interesting to see the differences among students.

—Jessica Rogers (Teacher)

I liked your cube, and I thought that it was very clear that you used all six different areas of thinking from Bloom's.

—Emily (Colleague)

I will have to read this essay! It sounds like something that my kids would love to read. I liked your cube. I think the questions you asked would be fun for the kids to answer and would also help them with comprehension.

—Suzanne (Colleague)

This sounds like a great essay and activity!

—Barbara (Colleague)

I too have students who don't like to write (and some are high-ability students). You might mix up the writing activities so students don't feel like they are writing so much. For example, let them create a comic strip (which contains writing, but also art), or let them create a trivia game about the story. This seems to help those students who don't enjoy the traditional ("Take out a piece of paper and write your answers in complete sentences") type of writing.

—Christina (Colleague)

Steps of the Writing Process Cubes
Verbs: Part 1

RECALL

Explain

Discuss

Identify

Illustrate

Summarize

Steps of the Writing Process Cubes
Writing Process: Part 1

Examples of transitions for:
- personal narratives
- descriptions
- comparisons/ contrasts
- persuasive writing

What makes a good writing topic

The traits of writing

The stages in the writing process

How a writer can hold his/her readers' interest

How a writer writes with voice

Differentiation That Really Works: Language Arts (Grades 6–12) © Taylor & Francis • Permission is granted to photocopy or reproduce this page for classroom use only.

Steps of the Writing Process Cubes
Verbs: Part 2

SHOW	**Decide**
EVALUATE / **Examine**	**Compare and Contrast**
Debate	

Created by Susan Schweitzer

Steps of the Writing Process Cubes
Writing Process: Part 2

The responder's role in peer editing

What a writer would check for when checking grammar (give specific examples)

What a writer would check for when checking punctuation (give specific examples)

How words affect the feeling of a writer's writing

How a writer can improve sentence style (give specific techniques)

What sentence structures writers should avoid (give specific examples)

Differentiation That Really Works: Language Arts (Grades 6–12) © Taylor & Francis • Permission is granted to photocopy or reproduce this page for classroom use only.

Real Teacher Comments

I created my cubing activity in two parts to review the writing process with my seventh-grade English classes. Each part consists of two cubes—one cube with verbs and one cube with statements. Using Bloom's verbs, Part 1 has knowledge and comprehension verbs, and Part 2 has application, analysis, and evaluation verbs. I couldn't come up with synthesis verbs that would apply to all of the statements on the other cubes, so I didn't include that level. Part 1 cubes were copied in yellow and Part 2 cubes were copied in green.

I alternated the sets of cubes as I distributed them around the room to groups of three students. Group 1 received Part 1 cubes, Group 2 received Part 2 cubes, Group 3 received Part 1 cubes, Group 4 received Part 2 cubes, and so on. I set the timer for 12 minutes. When it went off, the groups passed their cubes clockwise around the room. That way, every group was able to review both Part 1 and Part 2. They had time to play three rounds.

The 12-minute rounds seemed to work just fine. This review came after a month of working with the writing process, so the students really seemed to know the information. Students who attended our school last year did wonderfully, because they worked on the writing process all last year. However, students new to the school seemed to struggle a bit even though I had reminded them the day before to review their notes for an upcoming quiz on Tuesday. The cubing activity was a surprise on Friday.

I considered laminating the sheets of paper but was concerned that they wouldn't last long. I found plastic cubes (2.75" × 2.75") in the bridal isle at JoAnn Fabrics. They are frosted, but each side has a clear heart in its center, which frames the verbs and the statements. The students chuckled a bit [about the hearts] but enjoyed the review nonetheless. Because the cubes are plastic and fold flat, I will be able to reuse them.

—Susan Schweitzer (Teacher)

Thanks for the plastic cube idea! I was also looking around for some things I could use that would last longer than the laminated paper. The fact that they fold flat makes it even better! I really like the two different cubes that you created. Having the different cubes really adds to the functionality of the activity.

—Julia (Colleague)

I like your cube for writing, especially the Part 1 cube for the writing process, which describes the traits of (good) writing. Students are often not sure what they should write about or how they start writing. Your cube is so realistic and helpful for the students. It is well constructed.

—Jongkoo (Colleague)

The Boy in the Striped Pajamas Cube

List two different occasions on which Bruno showed extreme ignorance of Shmuel's situation.

Explain one way in which Bruno made a mistake and then took steps to fix it.

Bruno experienced several tense moments throughout the book. Pick one and explain how you **relate** to it.

Break the plot down into 3–5 sections. Where would each begin and end, and what would you call them?

Evaluate the novel: Was it an appropriate choice for your class? Give three strong reasons for or against it.

One theme of the novel is that ignorance can have disastrous consequences. What is one way that lesson could **apply** to middle school students?

Real Teacher Comments

This activity came at a good time, because my class has just finished John Boyne's novel *The Boy in the Striped Pajamas*. They'd already written several short essays as an assessment, but this cubing activity allowed me to cover a few more points of literary analysis. I put them in groups of three and instructed them to pretend that they were in an interview while answering the questions (no giggling, no using words like "um" and "well" as fillers, and so on). I told them that it was all right to pause while thinking of an answer. They had 15 minutes to take turns rolling the cube, so they all got to answer several questions. There was still a little giggling, as I expected from this group, but I also saw some good effort. I like that the activity allowed them to practice their speaking skills.

—Tracy Schwerin (Teacher)

I really liked how you used this to go along with the novel your class read. I think I will do something similar to this with my class. I read them a chapter every day from a novel, but I would like to make it more meaningful than just reading them a novel that they enjoy. They still love being read to at this age, but using the cube to go along with it either after each novel or as we go through the book might help hold them accountable for what I'm reading, along with helping them work on their listening skills!

—Rachel (Colleague)

CHAPTER 5
GRAPHIC ORGANIZERS

Overview

Graphic organizers are visual tools used by teachers to assist students in analyzing, interpreting, and making sense of the content. Graphic organizers come in many forms, depending on the use. Examples include Venn diagrams, compare/contrast charts, double bubble diagrams, and flow charts. Graphic organizers can be used as advanced organizers, sense-making activities, or as formative or summative assessments.

How and When to Use Graphic Organizers

Graphic organizers often are used as advanced organizers at the beginning of a lesson or activity to assist students in understanding the content. They also may be used for practice with activities that require students to make sense of the content. The teacher might choose to use graphic organizers to gather formative or summative data. To accommodate the needs of all learners, some organizers may be blank, while others may be partially completed, depending on the readiness level of the students.

Directions for Making Graphic Organizers

Graphic organizers are simple to design. However, there is no set template. The form and function of the graphic organizer will depend on the topic being taught, as well as the thinking skills students will be using. Inspiration®

 DOI: 10.4324/9781003234647-5

is one type of software that can be used to create graphic organizers (http://www.inspiration.com).

How This Strategy Fits in the CIRCLE MAP

When used for assessment purposes, graphic organizers fit in the "differentiated assessment" component of the CIRCLE MAP. However, when used as an advanced organizer or sense-making activity, they fit in the "differentiated instructional strategies" component.

Examples

The examples we have chosen include specific graphic organizers, as well as those that can be readily adapted to many topics. These organizers were created by real teachers who used them in their own classrooms. When possible, we have included the comments from the teachers and their colleagues with the intention that the comments may provide additional insight to using the organizers.

For example, in Dr. Bennett's eighth-grade English class, the students are reviewing cause and effect in three stories they have read. He has designed a graphic organizer to assist the students in identifying these elements. The graphic organizer has two boxes in each of four rows. In each case, an arrow points from the box on the left (Cause) to the box on the right (Effect). Dr. Bennett provides the names of the three stories from which students may choose for the activity. Students complete the graphic organizer while he walks around the room to get a good idea of which students seem to have mastered the concept and who might still need some reteaching. Once the students have completed the graphic organizers, he has them move into groups based on the story they used to complete the activity to share their results.

Template

Due to the nature of graphic organizers, there is no universal template.

Name:_____ Date:_____

English 10
This activity focuses on "Time Enough at Last," an episode
from Season 1 of *The Twilight Zone* (1959–1964).

What Gives Life Meaning?

Directions: In your own experience, what kind of things do you value most? What would you miss if those things were lost or taken from you? Complete the map below in which you list some of these things.

In the center circle, you should list your topic ("What I Would Miss" or "What I Need"). In each box, list something you would miss. Be sure to use complete sentences.

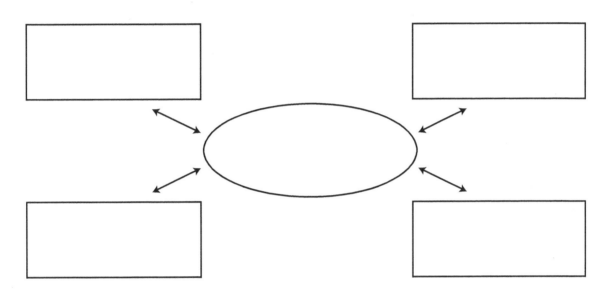

In one complete paragraph (approximately five sentences), discuss your "favorite things." Why are they important?

_____

_____

_____

_____

_____

_____

_____

As You View . . .

1. What are Henry Bemis's feelings:

Prior to the bombing?	Afterward?

2. The creator of this TV show, Rod Serling, inserts many symbols or examples of how we as humans are dependent upon commerce, and also of how we tend to promote anti-intellectualism. List two examples of such symbols.

_____

_____

3. How is the ending of this episode ironic?

_____

_____

What did Henry want?	What happened?

Created by Ami Brown

Real Teacher Comments

My sophomore students are currently working on a science fiction unit. We read a variety of selections from their textbook. I always like to supplement their readings with videos or other outside material. During our unit, we watched an episode from *The Twilight Zone* (the original series) called "Time Enough at Last." Before showing the episode, I have students discuss and complete a map in which they think about what matters most. This relates well to the episode, because the main character in the show wants to read more than anything else. He finally gets the "time" to do this when a nuclear bomb destroys his city. He is the only one left. He finds the library still intact, but alas, just as he is getting ready to read a book, his glasses fall off and break.

It was interesting to see what some of my students listed as being important to them. I had some really good responses, but there were also a few that were a bit telling of students' ages. I guess when you are 15 or 16 years old, the world isn't quite as complicated.

The rest of the graphic organizer helped me determine each student's level of understanding. Based on their responses, I was able to provide assistance to students who did not understand the use of symbols or the meaning of the word "ironic."

—Ami Brown (Teacher)

The Canterbury Tales: Moral Thermometer

Directions:

Rank each of the characters listed below based on his or her moral character. Consider all of the things that Chaucer says about them in the Prologue, in addition to details revealed about them in their tales.

- Rank the Parson, the Friar, the Nun, the Priest, the Pardoner, the Monk, the Wife of Bath, and the Summoner, writing their names in the corresponding boxes.

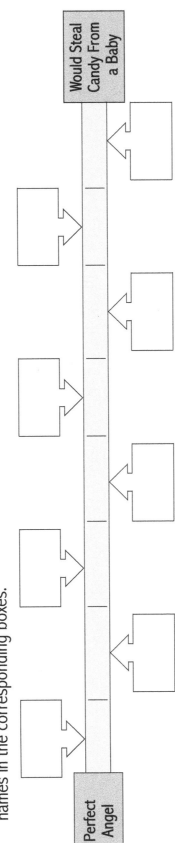

Would Steal Candy From a Baby

Perfect Angel

- Be prepared to defend your choices in class tomorrow (note examples for each character that led to your conclusion).
- Consider what Chaucer's descriptions of the characters, as a whole, reveal about his opinion of society.

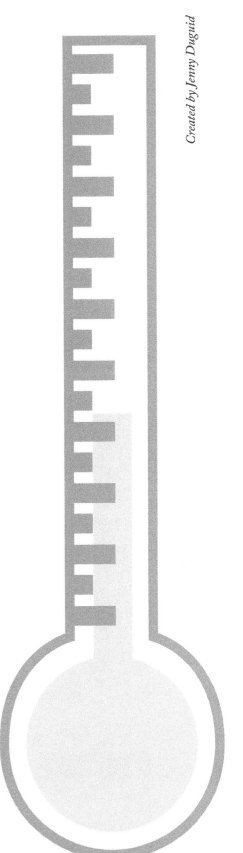

Created by Jenny Duguid

Real Teacher Comments

We finished up *The Canterbury Tales* last week, so to further push my students in their analysis and to tie our reading back into our study of the history of the time period, I asked them to rank characters on a "moral thermometer." I had to explain how it worked and then do an example with them (the organizer is not really self-explanatory); then I had them complete it as homework. We had an excellent discussion the next day, and they came to class prepared to really defend their opinions. From this activity they also made some great inferences about Chaucer's opinions of the church and the rising middle class. I was really pleased with how a fairly simple (in format) organizer could inspire so much higher order thinking.

—Jenny Duguid (Teacher)

The thermometer idea is such a great way to have students evaluate—a great higher level thinking activity—and to encourage them to defend their position is wonderful. I think this type of organizer could help students with lots of things, from very simple concepts all the way up to this complex concept you've presented. I was thinking about how cool it could be to give students a list of animals and a given habitat and have them place them on the continuum based on how well they would survive. Again, they'd need to defend their answers. It would also be a great way to gain insight into a student's thought processes if you asked the student to do something as simple as place math problems on the thermometer from easiest to hardest, justifying the problems' placement.

—Mona (Colleague)

What an outstanding idea! I loved studying Chaucer and *The Canterbury Tales*, both in high school and in college. My teachers and professors brought great life to our study of Chaucer and the time period in which he lived, making us excited to learn. You have done the same for your students by asking them to apply critical thinking skills. Oh, how I wish I could have been in your classroom to hear their discussion! It appears that you bring great life and enthusiasm to your classroom.

—Susan (Colleague)

Graphic Organizer for Plot Analysis

Somebody

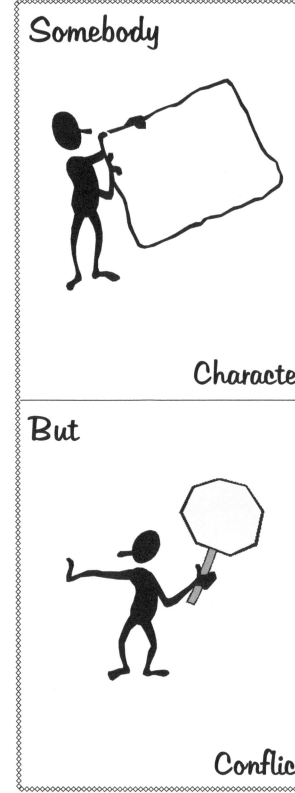

Character

Wanted

Motivation

But

Conflict

So

Resolution

Created by Amanda Fisher

Real Teacher Comments

I use this with all of my students to help them understand the complexities of plot. Many times they get stuck on trying to find "the" conflict. This graphic organizer helps them understand that there are many conflicts involved in a single story. For example, we could explore the tale of Cinderella: She *wanted* to go to the ball, *but* she didn't have a dress, *so* her fairy godmother came and made her one. The *prince* wanted to marry his mystery lady, *but* he couldn't find her, *so* he sent his soldiers to search the kingdom for the woman whose foot would fit into the glass slipper.

The great thing about it is that it can be adapted to any content area. For example, fractions (*somebody*), *want* to be added together, *but* they have different denominators, *so* we need to find a common denominator. The kids like it because it's simple and it helps them get down to the main point of the reading.

—Amanda Fisher (Teacher)

Name:_____ Date:_____

Vocabulary Graphic Organizer

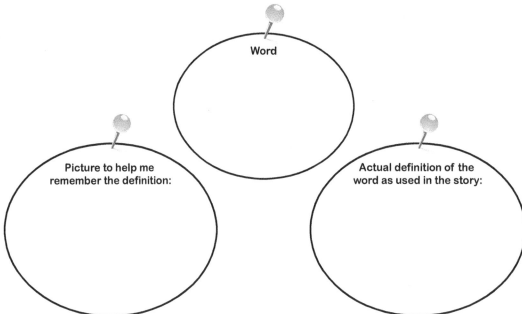

Word

Picture to help me
remember the definition:

Actual definition of the
word as used in the story:

Sentence from the story that uses this word:

My own sentence that uses this word:

Created by Suzanne Jones

Real Teacher Comments

I used this vocabulary graphic organizer with my advanced sixth-grade language arts classes. I had used something similar before, but it was too small and had too many different parts for the students to complete. They dreaded using it. I took the most important parts—the word, the picture the students create to help them remember the word, the definition, the sentence from the story, and the sentence they write themselves using the word—and created a larger graphic organizer. I assigned different vocabulary words to the students and had them share their graphic organizers at their tables. The goal was to help others remember their words.

The class did well overall on the vocabulary test, but I think that they would do better if they each completed the graphic organizer for each vocabulary word. I'll shrink it down a bit next time and give each student six copies for their six words. Having them remember definitions using a picture really works! They love to show others their pictures, and during the test, I see them doodling to help themselves remember the definitions.

—Suzanne Jones (Teacher)

Your graphic organizer is a good way to make your students think about the word in several different ways. They are forced to use a couple of different resources to help them in their understanding.

—Alicia (Colleague)

You had a lot of strategies to help your students with the vocabulary. It was a great visual tool. You mentioned shrinking it down. For next time, you could make it the size of an index card and put the cards on a binder ring for students to use for studying.

—Roberta (Colleague)

We do some similar activities with spelling words, and I think that it would be great to use the organizer for that, as well as for vocabulary in different subject areas!

—Emily (Colleague)

I like this graphic organizer. Using pictures to help students remember vocabulary words is an interesting technique, and it sounds like you found it to be an effective tool for your students. Also, I like the idea of the students teaching each other their vocabulary words.

—Billie (Colleague)

MAKE YOUR OWN KITE

The author mentions six steps to make your own kite.
Use this flowchart to summarize the steps. Include only the main ideas.

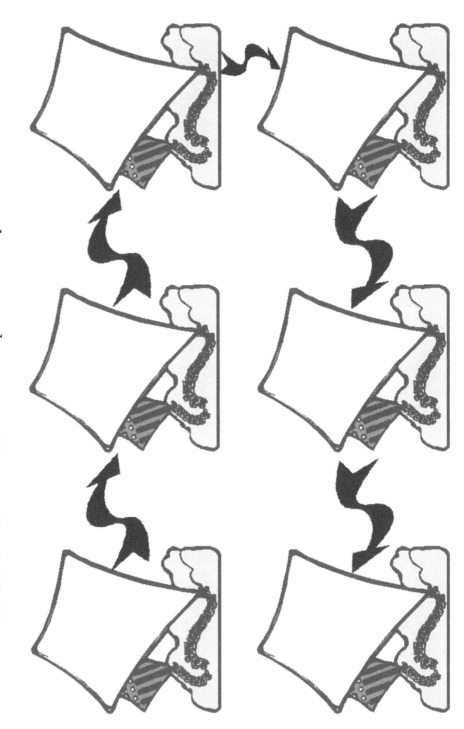

Real Teacher Comments

From the informational article we read in class, students were to write in order each step they would need to take to make their own kites. In addition, they needed to use summary skills, which we had studied previously.

The students liked that the graphic organizer went along with the theme of the article they had read. They also liked the arrows that showed the order in which they were to write the steps. Those who write with bigger letters did complain that they would have liked more room to write the steps, but overall, this graphic organizer was a hit with my students.

—Jessica Rogers (Teacher)

I like the kite pictures to go along with the story theme. It really laid out the steps nicely. I'm sure you got good information from this assignment.

—Christina (Colleague)

Students seem to remember a process so much better if they have pictures and break it down into clearly defined steps. I am sure your students will always remember how to make a kite.

—Nichole (Colleague)

What a great idea to help students work with summarizing and pulling out the main ideas. I like that you used a visual graphic related to the assignment.

—Amy (Colleague)

I loved this graphic organizer! You could use something similar for almost anything that includes giving directions in a specific order.

—Emily (Teacher)

I can think of several ways to adapt your graphic organizer. We have a science standard that states that students have to demonstrate how to write instructions. This would be a great way for the ideas to flow.

—Roberta (Colleague)

Vocabulary Square
Graphic Organizer

In your own words, what does the word mean?	Write three sentences using the word. In each sentence, use a different form of the word, if possible.

Word

_____

Write three meaningful nonexamples of the word.	Illustrate the word.

Created by Lisa Sarjeant

Real Teacher Comments

This is a graphic organizer my students use for tougher vocabulary words, usually those we encounter in reading or in other content areas. This week, the students are working on a consumer reports research project in which they research and recommend a technological device for their parents to buy, and they are finding a lot of technical words they don't know. So I handed out three copies of the vocabulary square graphic organizer to each student and asked students to find three unfamiliar words related to their technological devices.

My favorite quadrant on the square is the nonexample. The first time I gave this assignment, we had to spend some time discussing what is a meaningful nonexample and what is just silliness. Yes, "banana" is a nonexample of a lot of words, but we are looking for a word that exemplifies traits that are conspicuously **not** part of the original word's definition. For example, if the word is "balmy," a good nonexample is a snowstorm.

I enjoyed seeing the variety of vocabulary words they came up with for this particular assignment: LCD, gameplay, Bluetooth, fascia, polyphonic, tariff, shutter lag, ambient, bitrate . . . many I did not know myself!

—Lisa Sarjeant (Teacher)

I do think this is a valuable tool for developing vocabulary. I like the idea of the nonexample. I guess it's almost like thinking of an opposite. I will consider adding that box for some of my students who have more advanced vocabularies. Sometimes coming up with antonyms just doesn't work for some words, but coming up with a nonexample would be a good alternative.

—Daniel (Colleague)

This activity looks like it would get some higher thinking going by asking for three sentences using the words.

—Robert (Colleague)

Name: _____

Date: _____

COMMAS GRAPHIC ORGANIZER

Directions: Using the accompanying sheet of sentences, find two sentences that demonstrate each comma rule. Write those two sentences beneath the correct rule, and insert commas in the correct places. For the third sentence in every box, write a sentence of your own that demonstrates the rule, and insert commas in the correct places.

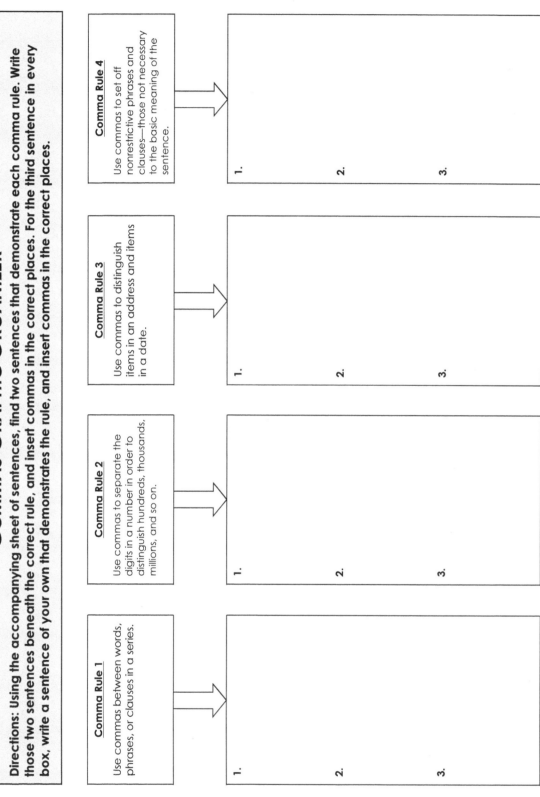

Comma Rule 1

Use commas between words, phrases, or clauses in a series.

1.

2.

3.

Comma Rule 2

Use commas to separate the digits in a number in order to distinguish hundreds, thousands, millions, and so on.

1.

2.

3.

Comma Rule 3

Use commas to distinguish items in an address and items in a date.

1.

2.

3.

Comma Rule 4

Use commas to set off nonrestrictive phrases and clauses—those not necessary to the basic meaning of the sentence.

1.

2.

3.

Created by Susan Schweitzer

Name: _____

Date: _____

COMMAS GRAPHIC ORGANIZER (CONTINUED)

Comma Rule 5

Use commas to set off a title, a name, or initials that follow a person's last name.

→

1.

2.

3.

Comma Rule 6

Use commas to set off a word, phrase, or clause that interrupts the main thought of a sentence.

→

1.

2.

3.

Comma Rule 7

Commas set off an appositive from the rest of the sentence. An appositive is a word or phrase that identifies a noun or pronoun.

→

1.

2.

3.

Comma Rule 8

Use commas to separate two or more adjectives that equally modify the same noun.

→

1.

2.

3.

Created by Susan Schweitzer

Name: _____

Date: _____

Commas Graphic Organizer (Continued)

Comma Rule 9
Use commas to set off the exact words of a speaker from the rest of the sentence.

1.

2.

3.

Comma Rule 10
Use commas to separate a noun of direct address from the rest of the sentence.

1.

2.

3.

Comma Rule 11
Use commas to separate an interjection or weak exclamation from the rest of the sentence.

1.

2.

3.

Comma Rule 12
Use commas to separate an explanatory phrase from the rest of the sentence.

1.

2.

3.

Name: _____

Date: _____

COMMAS GRAPHIC ORGANIZER (CONTINUED)

Comma Rule 13

Use a comma to separate an adverb clause or a long phrase from the independent clause that follows it.

1.

2.

3.

Comma Rule 14

Use a comma between two independent clauses that are joined by a coordinating conjunction (such as *and, but, or, nor, for, so,* and *yet*), forming a compound sentence. An independent clause expresses a complete thought and can stand alone as a sentence.

1.

2.

3.

Created by Susan Schweitzer

Practice Sentences for Comma Rules Graphic Organizer

Directions: Use the following sentences to complete the Comma Rules Graphic Organizer.

1. Well she opened a school in Nevada.
2. The Rio Grande one of the major rivers in North America forms part of the border between Texas and Mexico.
3. Today there are approximately 50000 bison in North America.
4. The *Wizard of Oz* which I saw again last week is my favorite movie.
5. Orbiting around the sun nine planets make up our solar system.
6. Like New York Chicago has a very active theater scene.
7. Tobacco hammock canoe and barbecue are a few of the many words that English-speaking people owe to Mexicans.
8. Grandmother threw the dirty unusable notebook in the garbage.
9. The musical comedy originated in America and it has retained a distinctly American flavor.
10. Be sure to mail your entry by December 1 2011 in order to receive your free gift.
11. Because Tiger Woods has won so many tournaments he also can make money from product endorsements.
12. William Tren Ph.D. wrote the article about the effects of video games on young children.
13. At the end of the report the student included a Works Cited page.
14. If it can be arranged the teacher announced we will visit the United Nations next Thursday.
15. The plane will fly into Nashville Tennessee and then return to Boston Massachusetts.
16. I hope to win the writing contest too.
17. To be honest I thought the movie was terrific.
18. Pamela found a shiny new penny when she was walking her dog.
19. The girl a student in Mrs. Schweitzer's eighth-hour class read 25 books before the end of the summer.
20. Because Ryan hit a home run his team won the baseball game.
21. By the end of study hall the students had completed all of their homework.
22. The last school day for students is June 3 2011 if there are no make-up days.
23. The article about endangered species was written by James O'Connor D.V.M.
24. The seventh-grade teachers as you can imagine are badly in need of a vacation.
25. No Tammy I have not read your report about whales yet.

26. The population of Schererville is approximately 28886 people.

27. The majority of the world's water supply 98 percent of it comes from the oceans.

28. The students however are looking forward to the picnic the most.

29. Melanie's favorite flavors of ice cream are strawberry chocolate and mint.

30. All sixth graders read *Castle in the Attic* but all seventh graders read *The Outsiders*.

31. The flight leaves Chicago Illinois at 4:30 P.M. and arrives in Orlando Florida at 8:30 P.M.

32. You must said Julian return that book to the library before it closes.

33. Unlike Justin the rest of the class remained quiet while the teacher was talking.

34. Running through the hallways the boys tripped and scattered their book everywhere.

35. Many huge ships cruise liners and cargo freighters provide people with opportunities for both work and play.

36. My sister listening to the radio did not hear me call her for dinner.

Created by Susan Schweitzer

Real Teacher Comments

I created a graphic organizer for the comma rules found in [the textbook my students use]. Both the text I use with my seventh-grade students and the text I use with my gifted seventh-grade students have the same 14 rules.

For my general education students, I used the graphic organizer as a review at the end of our comma unit. Each teacher-selected group of three students included a high-, average-, and low-ability student. Where groups of four were necessary, I tried to include two average-ability students along with a high-ability and low-ability student. It took the groups three class periods to complete the graphic organizer. In some cases I had to intervene and guide them. However, because it was at the end of the unit, most groups were able to complete the graphic organizer with little assistance from me. The next step for these students will be a summative test.

With my gifted seventh-grade students, I used the graphic organizer as a preassessment tool, so they completed the activity individually. It took the majority of the students two class periods to complete the activity. The students were able to complete the activity with satisfactory results. Next, students will begin a unit of study during which they will only review the rules that caused them trouble. Each student will be given exercises to complete in order to review their problem areas.

—Susan Schweitzer (Teacher)

I love your graphic organizer using commas. One of our standards involves using commas. I will be able to easily implement your graphic organizer into my unit. Thanks for sharing!

—Shannon (Colleague)

I really like this graphic organizer. I'm thankful that it can be easily tailored to another grade level, as well as another subject area. I love how it has the students put their learning into practice by having them first pick out sentences that follow a rule, then create their own.

—Julia (Colleague)

CHAPTER 6

LEARNING CONTRACTS

Overview

Learning contracts are "bargains" between the teacher and a student or group of students. Learning contracts may be on any topic and may be considered abbreviated lesson plans or mini-units. That is, learning contracts list standards, concepts, goals, activities, resources, products, and assessments in a format that is student-friendly. They have a starting and ending date and a place for the student, the teacher, and the student's parents to sign indicating that the contract is binding. Generally, learning contracts are used as an alternative to regular instruction, especially when students have been compacted out of a portion of the curriculum.

How and When to Use Learning Contracts

In a classroom, the learners are at a variety of readiness levels. To accommodate these differences, many teachers begin a unit of instruction by pretesting the entire class on the planned content. Some students already may know significant portions of the content and need alternative activities while the rest of the class proceeds with learning the content that is new to them. To provide clearly articulated learning experiences for the students who already have mastered the planned content, a learning contract often is an appropriate choice. Generally, the student and teacher jointly plan the contract, agree to the terms, and sign it. In our experience, it also is vital that parents sign the contract to avoid unnecessary miscommunication.

 DOI: 10.4324/9781003234647-6

Directions for Making Learning Contracts

Learning contracts are simple to create using the template provided on the next page. However, it is easy to design your own learning contract customized to a particular topic. Any learning contract should include all of the elements of the template.

How This Strategy fits in the CIRCLE MAP

A learning contract fits in the "differentiated instructional strategies" component of the CIRCLE MAP. Learning contracts are generally alternative assignments used to accommodate individual or small-group rather than whole-class learning needs.

Examples

The examples we have chosen all use the template but address different topics. These contracts were created by real teachers who used them in their own classrooms. When possible, we have included the comments from the teachers and their colleagues with the intention that the comments may provide additional insight to using the learning contract and for creating your own or another topic.

For example, Savion, Sylvia, and Avery are students in Catherine Callahan's honors seventh-grade English class. The next topic is poetry. On a pretest over that topic, Mrs. Callahan found that most of her class had only rudimentary knowledge about types of poetry and either a neutral or a poor attitude towards it. The exceptions were Savion, Sylvia, and Avery. All three scored 97–100% on the pretest and indicated a positive or very positive attitude towards poetry. Mrs. Callahan met with the three students to discuss possible options for a learning contract for their use during the time the other students would be working through the poetry unit. These students were very interested in ancient poetry and poetry of the Middle Ages. Mrs. Callahan helped the students identify books, videos, and websites that would be helpful. She keyed the objectives to the state standards and developed the contract, making sure to include checkpoints to be sure the students were on target with their independent work. The students would learn about poetry of these eras and write some of their own based on the formats they had studied. Once developed, each contract was signed by the student, the student's parents, and Mrs. Callahan.

Template

Title of Learning Contract

Standards:

Goals/Objectives:

Topic:

Activities:

Resources:

Product/Outcome:

Evaluation Criteria:

Signatures:

Student: _____   Teacher: _____

Parent: _____   Date: _____

The Truth That We Know: The "Story" Behind the Tale of *Animal Farm*

Standards:

- Plan and conduct multiple-step information searches by using computer networks.
- Achieve an effective balance between researched information and original ideas.
- Use a computer to create documents by using word-processing skills and publishing programs; develop simple databases and spreadsheets to manage information and prepare reports.
- Write research reports that define a thesis (statement of position on the topic); include important ideas, concepts, and direct quotations from significant information sources, including print reference materials and the Internet, and paraphrase and summarize all perspectives on the topic as appropriate; use a variety of primary and secondary sources and distinguish the nature and value of each; organize and display information on charts, tables, and graphs; and document sources with reference notes and a bibliography.
- Edit and proofread own writing as well as that of others, using an editing checklist or set of rules, with specific examples and corrections of frequent errors.
- Deliver research presentations that define a thesis (a position on the topic); research important ideas, concepts, and direct quotations from significant information sources and paraphrase and summarize important perspectives on the topic; and use a variety of research sources and distinguish the nature and value of each.

Topic: Background/historical investigation on *Animal Farm*, the Russian Revolution, and communism

Goals:

1. Students will select a historical "parallel" to research.
2. Students will work together to investigate pertinent information that identifies a correlation between *Animal Farm* and their parallel topic.
3. Students will present their research in a multimedia format.
4. Students will write an essay in which they summarize their findings. Students will identify the relationship between their topics and the events in the novel *Animal Farm*.

Activities:

1. In groups of three, select **one** of the following topics to research. Use the questions to guide you.
   - **Karl Marx (the "father" of communism).** What social conditions promoted the popularity of this ideology?

- **Czar Nicholas II and the Russian Revolution.** What was society like during this time? How might the Czar have contributed to the revolution?
- **Lenin and the Russian Revolution.** What ideas did Lenin promote? What were his intentions (e.g., to help people, to gain power)?
- **Stalin.** How did life change under his rule? What was occurring within society at this time?
- **Communism as a form of government.** How is it different from ours? Is it all bad? All good?

2. Complete a graphic organizer (provided by your teacher) related to your topic. The organizer will help you not only to brainstorm ideas related to your topic, but also to disseminate information among your group members.

> You will need to generate at least three different areas to investigate within your topic. Each person will be responsible for one particular area of focus.

3. Complete a source information sheet for at least three sources related to your area of focus. The source information sheet will help you keep track of your sources. It will also allow you to determine important ideas, quotes, figures, and so on related to your particular area of focus. You may choose to include sources from the Internet or other materials. Make sure your sources are credible.
4. Using your source information sheet, create an outline and a rough draft for your essay response. The rough draft should include an effective introduction, body, and conclusion. You will also need to have a thesis statement that centers on a particular idea that you have found to be important in relation to your topic.
5. Within your group, create a multimedia presentation of your research using PowerPoint. This presentation should not only describe your findings, but it must also show some correlation with *Animal Farm*. Your presentation should last approximately 10 minutes.
6. Review drafts with me and within your groups using the peer editing checklist. Complete a final copy and include a bibliography that lists all sources. Use MLA format in your work. Your final essay should be three pages in length.

Due Dates:

Graphic organizer due
    for review: _____

Source sheet due
    for review: _____

Outline/rough
    draft due: _____

Peer editing
    checklist due: _____

Presentation
    due: _____

Final copy
    of essay due: _____

Check for Understanding

Please let me know if you do not understand the steps involved or their due dates. I will periodically remind you of upcoming requirements. **Please** ask questions!

Signatures:

I understand the above-listed requirements, and I will do my best to complete them on time.

Student: _____

Parent: _____

Teacher: _____

Created by Ami Brown

Real Teacher Comments

My eighth-grade honors students are required to read *Animal Farm*. One of my favorite aspects of teaching this novel is studying the relationship between the book and history. I really love the parallels and Orwell's use of allegory.

My learning contract covers a research project that students are required to complete as part of this novel study. I have done this project in the past, but I have never used a learning contract. I know it will make life much simpler for all. This contract makes the steps so clear, and it's much easier to know what is due when. I see the contract as a guide, and my job as a teacher is to give instruction along the way. I show them how to do it, and the contract shows them what they need to do and when.

—Ami Brown (Teacher)

Learning Contract

Name: John Doe
Subject: English (Literary Movements)
Start Date: _____ Due Date: _____

Standards:

- Analyze ways in which poets use imagery, personification, figures of speech, and sounds to evoke readers' emotions.
- Analyze and evaluate works of literary or cultural significance in American, English, or world history that reflect a variety of genres in the respective major periods in literature; were written by important authors in each historical period; reveal contrasts in major themes, styles, and trends in these historical periods; and reflect or shed light on the seminal philosophical, religious, social, political, or ethical ideas of their time.

Goals/Objectives:

- Students will analyze a variety of poetry representative of the Romantic period, including work by Blake, Burns, Shelley, Byron, and Keats.
- Students will be able to identify key characteristics that illustrate the style of each author.
- Students will be able to identify examples of imagery, sound to evoke emotion, symbolism, and musical devices (onomatopoeia, assonance, consonance, and rhyme).
- Students will understand that:
  - The time period during which a poet writes helps to shape the poet's style and beliefs.
  - Although they all are considered Romantic poets, each poet during this time had an individual style.
  - The name "Romantic" can be misleading, as it has little to do with love.

Topic: Romantic poetry

Activities:

- This learning contract will be used with students who already demonstrate mastery in identifying poetry elements (imagery, sound to evoke emotion, symbolism, and so on).
- All students will participate in the introductory activities about the Romantic period and Romantic authors (general information). Students who demonstrate mastery on a preassessment will then work independently on a learning contract analyzing the work of Romantic authors.

Students Will:

1. Select two authors of the Romantic period.
2. Research biographical information about the two authors, as well as information about each author's individual style.

3. Read work by both authors and select a poem from each that is indicative of that particular author's style.

4. Explicate each poem, identifying poetry elements, Romantic poetry elements, and elements of that author's particular style.

5. Compare and contrast the style of the two Romantic authors. How are they similar, and how are they different?

See Product/Outcome for final analysis formatting.

Resources:

- http://www.englishhistory.net
  Biographical information and poetry of Byron and Keats
- http://www.online-literature.com
  Biographical information and poetry of all Romantic poets
- http://www.poetryfoundation.org
  Biographical information and poetry of all Romantic poets
- Print resources can also be accessed at the school media center.

Product/Outcome:

The final analysis/comparison of the two poems/authors may be presented in the following formats:

- a formal essay,
- a PowerPoint presentation,
- a poster board, or
- another format approved by the teacher.

Evaluation Criteria:

Please see the Romantic poet rubric sample at http://www.rcampus.com/rubricshowc.cfm?code=T436X6&sp=true.

In signing this contract, I acknowledge that I will be working independently on my project during class time. Before leaving the classroom, I will get teacher permission. I will come to class each day with something to work on and will not disturb my fellow classmates. This project is due on the date specified at the top of the form.

Signatures:

Student: _____

Teacher: _____

Parent: _____

Created by Jenny Duguid

Real Teacher Comments

This is a contract that I would use with my next unit on Romantic poetry. It's designed for students who are above grade level in their poetry analysis. They still get to see a sampling of Romantic poets, and they still get the same background about the time period, but they are working on a more collegiate level, with higher order thinking and analysis skills. My biggest concern in coming up with a learning contract for high school students is making sure at the beginning that they understand their boundaries and the expectation that they come to class every day with something to do (otherwise, they will show up ready to nap or goof off). I think it's an excellent idea to get parental signatures—especially with older kids, who love to procrastinate.

—Jenny Duguid (Teacher)

Although I don't teach high school, I understand your concern [about students goofing off if they do not come to class prepared to work]. I teach middle school, and my biggest concern was similar. I was worried that students would feel lost or spend long amounts of time doing one small task without moving on. I'm not really familiar with what might work for high school, but I decided to break my learning contract into three parts. My students will have to turn in evidence of their work for each part of the contract. I thought that would allow for nice little checkpoints where they could make sure they were on the right track. I hope it works!

—Laura (Colleague)

Learning Contract:
Grade 8

|||||||||||||||||||||||||||||||||||||||||||||||||||||||||||||||||||||||||||||||||||||||||||||||||||||||||||||

Name: Zoe
Subject: English
Start Date: _____ Due Date: _____

Standards:

- Determine and articulate the relationship between the purposes and characteristics of different forms of poetry, including ballads, lyrics, couplets, epics, elegies, odes, and sonnets.
- Identify significant literary devices, such as metaphor, symbolism, dialect or quotations, and irony, which define a writer's style, and use those elements to interpret the work.
- Zoe has an above-grade-level understanding of these standards and has already had two original poems published in a school literary magazine.

Goals/Objectives:

Zoe will . . .

- compare and contrast poets and poems;
- explore the concepts of meter, rhythm, and flow; and
- expand knowledge of poets by researching different poets and their works.

Topic:

Poetry

Activities:

1. Research at least five poets whom you find personally interesting. Locate biographical information and find text for some of the authors' better known works. Explore poets from a variety of time periods, backgrounds, beliefs, and subject matters.
2. Compare the poets' treatment of topic, theme, format, and bibliographical background.
3. Look at the use of literary elements to convey theme and style.
4. Write poetry on a similar topic or in a similar format/style.

Resources:

Internet, library, books, poetry anthologies

Product/Outcome:

Zoe will . . .

- create a visual comparison (e.g., Venn diagram, picture) of poems' formats, poems' themes, and poets' backgrounds;
- write at least five poems in similar formats to or on similar topics as poems she has read, at least one poem per poet; and
- write a personal reflection on what she has learned and how she feels she has benefitted from the opportunity.

Evaluation Criteria:

- completion of all requirements,
- similarities to the original poets' works,
- articulation of topic and theme, and
- personal reflection on material learned and benefits study.

Signatures:

Student: _____

Teacher: _____

Parent: _____

Created by Amanda Fisher

Real Teacher Comments

I wrote this contract for my poetry unit. This year I have a girl who has already read nearly all of Emily Dickinson's work and is familiar with Virginia Woolf, as well as the work of several other famous authors. So I'm going to give her some freedom with the unit. I worked together with her to make this contract so that she can expand her poetry horizon in the areas she likes. I'm going to suggest that she look into T. S. Eliot and a few other poets. She is extremely excited about this. English is one of her passions, and I know she is looking forward to learning about topics that interest her without being held back by her peers.

—Amanda Fisher (Teacher)

Name:_____ Date:_____

Learning Contract for High-Ability Reading Group
The True Confessions of Charlotte Doyle

     This learning contract has been created for a particular reading group comprised of six students in grade 6. This group meets daily for 60–75 minutes. Students work independently with daily teacher check-ins. They are reading a different novel than the rest of the class. The novel was selected by both interest and readiness level and is recommended for grades 6–8. I am addressing the contract work to seventh-grade standards.

Subject: Reading/Language Arts

Standards:
- Understand and explain slight differences in meanings of related words.
- Understand text that uses a compare-contrast organizational pattern.
- Make reasonable statements and conclusions about a text, supporting them with accurate examples.
- Analyze the effect of the qualities of the character on the plot and the resolution of the character.
- Critique the believability of characters and the degree to which a plot is believable or realistic.
- Choose the form of writing that best suits the intended purpose.
- Restate and carry out multiple-step oral instructions and directions.
- Deliver presentations on problems and solutions that theorize on the causes and effects of each problem, establish connections between the defined problem and at least one solution, and offer persuasive evidence to support the definition of the problem and the proposed solutions.

Concept:
Change (i.e., how life in general, ideas, families, travel, and education have changed from the 1830s to today)

Goal/ Objectives:
Students will:
- read and understand the novel *The True Confessions of Charlotte Doyle*;
- understand some societal changes from 1800 to the present;
- gain knowledge of the workings of a brig, the names of masts, and the areas of the boat;
- gain knowledge of how a prim and proper young lady should behave;
- gain knowledge and practice in knot tying; and
- learn the prologue and the afterward as parts of a novel.

Activities:
Complete the required activities (noted with an asterisk) and choose two additional activities.
1. *Keep a daily journal (like Charlotte did) summarizing the daily events you read about in the novel. (knowledge, summary)
2. Using a model or drawing of the *Seahawk* as a visual aid, show and tell your classmates about Charlotte's life as a member of the crew. (application)
3. *Compare and contrast Charlotte's ship family to her biological family. Create a graphic organizer to show your information. (analysis)

4. *There are several father figures in this book. Choose two and explain how they are like a father to Charlotte. Cite specific examples and add your personal feelings to your explanation. Write a letter to each father figure. (analysis)

5. Learn how to tie at least four different knots used on the ship. Prepare a demonstration to teach other students how to tie these knots. Set up a learning center with step-by-step directions and illustrations. (application)

6. Discover how Avi, the author, creates a mood of mystery in the prologue and the first two chapters of *The True Confessions of Charlotte Doyle*. Lead a small-group discussion. (analysis)

7. Develop an idea for a game that will help new sailors learn how to live and work aboard a ship such as the *Seahawk*. Assemble a practice game and teach the group how to play. (synthesis)

8. *The True Confessions of Charlotte Doyle* is "decorated," not illustrated. Select the scene that, in your opinion, is most visually compelling, and make a charcoal drawing. On the back, outline your reasons for choosing this scene. (evaluation)

9. *Does Charlotte choose the right wind? Defend your conclusion in an Afterward for the novel. (evaluation)

Assessment:

- For the required activities, the 6 + 1 Trait® Writing rubric will be used to assess the writing.
- A special rubric will be designed specifically for each of the activity choices that are not required. For each of these activity choices, there will also be a peer evaluation form.
- Because the teacher meets with this group daily for small discussions, feedback, and monitoring work, the teacher will make formative judgments along the way as the novel is read.

Resources:

- Avi, *The True Confessions of Charlotte Doyle*, Orchard Books, 1990 (paperback copy for each student)
- Internet websites to investigate brigs and cargo ships from circa 1800
- Class visitor, knot-tying expert
- Classroom maps and atlases

Signature:

Student: _____

Teacher: _____

Parent: _____

Created by Chris Gesse

Real Teacher Comments

This is a novel study for high-ability sixth-grade students. I wanted to be sure I had plenty of options that would allow my students to use high-level thinking skills. There are enough options that students can choose activities that appeal to their interests and match their learning profiles in addition to completing the required activities. All of the students responded positively to the learning contract and have asked to have this option again.

—Chris Gesse (Teacher)

I like the number of choices you gave your students and how you noted the required activities with an asterisk. I also liked the range of difficulty that you provided.

—Melinda (Colleague)

Learning Contract

Name: John Q. Student
Subject: English 10 Honors
Start Date: _____ Due Date: _____

Standards:

- Analyze the structure and format of various informational documents and explain how authors use the features to achieve their purposes.
- Extend—through original analysis, evaluation, and elaboration—ideas presented in primary or secondary sources.
- Evaluate an author's argument or defense of a claim by examining the relationship between generalizations and evidence, the comprehensiveness of evidence, and the way in which the author's intent affects the structure and tone of the text.

Goals/Objectives:

- The student will analyze the language and intent of famous speeches.
- The student will compare and contrast the works of one selected author.
- The student will create an original product in homage to the selected author.

Topic:

Understanding and evaluating the tone of speeches given by Nobel laureates in literature

Activities:

Using the website http://nobelprize.org/nobel_prizes/literature, the student will peruse and select an author to study. An analysis of the banquet speech and other supplementary information will be used to gain a better understanding of the author. The student will then decide upon key points and factors that have visibly influenced the writing of the chosen author. The next step will require the reading and evaluation of a selection of the author's works. The goal is to find evidence from the career of the author that supports what is highlighted in the Nobel speech. After this has been completed, the student will create a work of writing or art that pays tribute to the author.

Resources:

- Internet access
- Library materials
- Novels/anthologies/collections
- Computer publishing software
- Artistic supplies

Product/Outcome:

Written or artistic homage to the selected author. Evident or visible connection to the subject should be made through a written summary that explains the author's purpose, selected works, claims in speech, support in career, tone, and breadth and depth of source readings.

Evaluation Criteria:

A rubric using the following criteria will be used:

- organization of ideas,
- originality,
- research/background,
- presentation, and
- analysis.

Signature:

Student: _____

Teacher: _____

Parent: _____

Created by Stephen Merkle

Real Teacher Comments

I want to provide some of my honors students with an individual option for a novel unit. This involves a study of one of the Nobel laureates in literature. I wanted the students to be able to use primary sources including speeches and original works. Rather than having the students write a traditional essay about the author, I developed this creative homage project. This incorporates high-level thinking skills to a greater extent.

—Stephen Merkle (Teacher)

Language Arts Learning Contract

Name: _____ Period: _____

Topic: Vocabulary

Start Date: _____ Due Date: _____

Standards:

- Verify the meaning of a word in its context, even when its meaning is not directly stated, through the use of definition, restatement, example, comparison, or contrast.
- Write using precise word choices to make writing interesting and exact.

Learning Objectives:

1. Integrate new vocabulary words fluidly into writing.
2. Identify patterns inside of and among words.
3. Define new vocabulary words.

Resources:

- *Sadlier-Oxford Vocabulary, Book Level C* or similar resource

Assignments:

1. Write an ongoing, cohesive story throughout the 9 weeks in which you use each vocabulary word from our list at least once. Underline the words as you use them.
2. Complete a word study for five words from each unit. Analyze prefixes, suffixes, roots, and related words.
3. Study for the final test.

Evaluation/Assessment:

1. The story will be graded according to your success in using each vocabulary word in the correct context in terms of both grammar and meaning.
2. The word study will be graded for accuracy and completion.
3. You must score an 85% or better on the final test.

Progress Checks:

Task	Date
Root study completion 20 words used in story	
Root study completion 20 additional words used in story	
Root study completion 20 additional words used in story	

Signatures:

This contract replaces regular class work for vocabulary. Your signature indicates your agreement to complete all work as listed.

Student: _____

Teacher: _____

Parent: _____

Created by Lisa Sarjeant

Real Teacher Comments

I made this for an individual student who loves creative writing and is bored by the vocabulary workbook we're using. I bumped him up one level in the vocabulary workbook, but he still hated completing the vocabulary exercises. We came up with this compromise: I let him fill in the dates for his progress check. He was really happy about getting to do something different from the rest of the classmates and for getting the chance to work on a long story, which he is often doing anyway. He told me the other day that his goal is to finish writing a book before his sophomore year.

—Lisa Sarjeant (Teacher)

Name:_____ Date:_____

Strategy: Learning Contract

Teacher: Susan Schweitzer   **Resource:** Student choice of novel
Subject: Reading   **Audience:** All students in class
Grade: Grade 7 Gifted   **Length of study:** 4 weeks
Topic: Independent novel study

Standards:
- Reading: Word Recognition, Fluency, and Vocabulary Development
  - Students use their knowledge of word parts and word relationships, as well as context, to determine the meaning of specialized vocabulary and to understand the precise meanings of grade-level-appropriate words.
- Reading: Comprehension and Analysis of Literary Text
  - Students read and respond to grade-level-appropriate historically or culturally significant works of literature.

Goals/Objectives:
- As a result of this learning contract, students will *know*:
  - that prior knowledge and experiences affect how they interact with literature, and
  - specialized vocabulary for this genre.
- As a result of this learning contract, students will *understand that*:
  - reading is an active process in which readers interact with the text to construct meaning within the context of their own understanding and experiences; and
  - readers use appropriate strategies and conventions to construct meaning before, during, and after reading.
- As a result of this learning contract, students will *be able to*:
  - identify story elements of the novel;
  - value reading as a means of learning and enjoyment;
  - read for a variety of purposes, including to gather information, to follow directions, to give a response, to form an opinion, to understand information, and to enjoy and appreciate;
  - read a range of contemporary and classical texts appropriate to their interests and learning needs; and
  - read texts from a variety of genres and cultural traditions.
- Students will demonstrate knowledge through self-selected activities.

Evaluation Criteria:
- Assessment will be in the form of:
  - successful completion of chosen activities as determined by the rubric for each activity,
  - teacher-and-student weekly meetings, and
  - up-to-date progress logs.
- Students will complete the contract in the allotted time.

Novel Study Learning Contract

Directions:

- Choose a novel set during World War II or the Holocaust that is at your reading level.
- Choose and complete activities to earn a total of 15 points.
- To earn the points, you must:
    - keep a log of your progress, including a timeline of your work;
    - meet with the teacher twice a week to discuss your progress log and timeline;
    - follow all directions for each activity;
    - complete all work neatly;
    - show details and use examples and information from the novel to demonstrate your understanding;
    - use correct spelling and grammar; and
    - do your best.

1-Point Activities:

1. Pick one scene from the novel and create a comic strip.
2. Write a one-page recommendation as to why the novel should or should not be read. Along with your reasons, cite evidence from the novel to support your comments.
3. Write a one-page letter to the author telling him or her what you liked and disliked about his or her novel and writing style. Along with your reasons, cite evidence from the novel to support your comments.
4. Create a Venn diagram comparing yourself to one of the characters.
5. Design a poster to advertise the novel.
6. Create a map to illustrate the setting of the novel.
7. Create a poem about the main character(s). Illustrate the poem.
8. Create a character map of the main character(s).
9. Write a paper in which you describe the funniest, saddest, happiest, most believable, and most unbelievable parts of the novel. Cite examples from the novel to support your feelings.
10. Write a newspaper article telling about the events in the novel. Make sure you include information telling who, what, where, when, why, and how.
11. Make a shoebox diorama depicting a scene from the novel. Write a paragraph to accompany the diorama.
12. Design your own 1-point project. (The teacher must approve your project.)

2-Point Activities:

1. Make a mobile with at least five people/places from the novel. Write a minimum of one paragraph explaining each piece.
2. Make a timeline of at least 10 events from the novel. Illustrate each item.
3. Create another character for the story. What would this character be like? How would the story change because of this character? Write a minimum of three paragraphs (the first paragraph should describe the new character, the second paragraph should answer the first question above, and the third paragraph should answer the second question above). Draw a picture of what this character looks like.
4. Create a story map of the novel. (See the teacher for sample story maps.)
5. Create a collage that celebrates the novel. Use pictures, words, and phrases to depict the main theme of the novel. Write a minimum of one paragraph to explain your collage.
6. Create a board game about the novel. Make cards that deal with information from the book.
7. Design your own 2-point project. (The teacher must approve your project.)

3-Point Activities:

1. Imagine that you are the main character. Keep a diary account of the daily events in the novel and explain what effect they had on you.
2. Write and perform a television commercial to sell the novel. The presentation may be in person or through a DVD. It must be 3 minutes long.
3. Write an additional chapter that tells what happens next after your novel ends.
4. Make a DVD with at least 10 scenes.
5. Design your own 3-point project. (The teacher must approve your project.)

Name:_____ Date:_____

Contract

I have chosen to read the following novel: _____
by _____ (date).

I understand that I must complete the novel and activities (totaling 15 points) between
the start date of _____ and the end date of _____.

I understand that my learning contract must be validated by three signatures.

I have chosen the following activities:

#	Activities	Points
		Total Points = 15

By signing this agreement, I agree to the terms and conditions set forth in this learning contract.

Signature:

Student: _____

Teacher: _____

Parent: _____

Created by Susan Schweitzer

Real Teacher Comments

As part of our Holocaust studies, my gifted language arts students study and explore the Kindertransport by reading *The Children of Willesden Lane*, by Mona Golabek and Lee Cohen. They explore issues related to this historical time period through poetry, art, and research about topics of personal interest. Additionally, students must select a novel of historical significance to read as one of the culminating projects. In the past, students were grouped according to interest. The members of the group read the same novel and participated in literature circle activities. I wanted to try a different approach this year and give students more choice of activities through which they could demonstrate their knowledge. I developed my learning contract with that goal in mind.

—Susan Schweitzer (Teacher)

Name:_____ Date:_____

LEARNING CONTRACT

Grade Level: 6

Subject: Language Arts

Standards:

- Identify different genres and discuss the major characteristics of each.
- Connect and clarify main ideas by identifying their relationships to multiple sources and related topics.
- Analyze the effect of the qualities of the character on the plot.
- Identify and analyze features of themes conveyed through characters, actions, and images.
- Write responses to literature focused around clear ideas.
- Ask questions that seek information not already discussed.

Topic: Greek mythology

Goals/Objectives:

1. Compare and contrast five Greek myths in order to identify the most common elements of character, plot, and theme.
2. Determine the 2–4 cultural values most important to the tellers of the Greek myths you've studied. Then pick one and speculate on its necessity to ancient Greek culture based on your current knowledge.

Time to Complete Tasks: 3 weeks

Activities:

1. Read each myth, taking notes on the character traits of both gods and humans, as well as on the basic plot and the themes taught through the actions of the characters. (After finishing a myth and its notes, your teacher will ask you to provide a brief oral summary of the myth, and then we will look over your notes together.)
2. Study your charts and circle common elements. Then write 2–4 statements (cultural values) you believe were important to the ancient Greeks.
3. Brainstorm what you know about Greek culture by creating a web.
4. Choose one of your statements that you believe to be particularly relevant to Greek culture. Write an essay of at least one typed page explaining why the acceptance of this value was essential to the Greek way of life. (Why did they pass this belief on to their children? How did it help maintain their lifestyle?)

Resources:
- Five blank character/plot/theme charts
- Selection of picture books/mythology collections from library

Products: Completed notes, statements, and essay

Evaluation/Assessment:
- Thoroughness of notes (careful observations, balance of information)
- Accuracy of statements based on notes
- Focus and clarity of essay, strength of sources and support

Created by Tracy Schwerin

Real Teacher Comments

This contract is designed for a gifted student who is currently struggling with motivation to complete homework assignments. Greek mythology is his area of strong interest and knowledge. I have found that using a child's interest to work on a weakness is a great way to help the child succeed.

—Tracy Schwerin (Teacher)

CHAPTER 7

TIERED LESSONS

Overview

According to Adams and Pierce (2006), tiered lessons are designed for all students to address the same academic standard or concept, but at varying levels of depth, complexity, or structure. Tomlinson (1999) indicated that tiered lessons are staples for differentiating instruction. Tiered lessons allow several pathways for students to arrive at an essential understanding based on the students' readiness. Erickson (2002) described essential understanding as "the key principles and generalizations that develop from the fact base. . . . They are the 'big ideas' that transfer through time and across cultures" (p. 47). Implementing a tiered lesson implies that the teacher has a good understanding of the students' ability levels with respect to the lesson and has developed the tiers to meet those needs. The number of tiers depends on the range of ability levels in the classroom.

How and When to Use Tiered Lessons

Use tiered lessons anytime you need students to work on similar material but at varying levels of readiness. Readiness can be reflected in skill level, reading level, or ability to handle multiple sets of directions, for example. As we noted before (Adams & Pierce, 2006), many examples of tiered lessons have three tiers: below grade level, at grade level, and above grade level. There is no rule that states there may only be three tiers, however. The number of tiers depends on the range of ability levels in the classroom. Remember: You will be forming tiers based on the assessment of your students' abilities to

 DOI: 10.4324/9781003234647-7

handle the material particular to the lesson. Students are regrouped when you decide to move to a different lesson. The number of groups per tier will vary, as will the number of students per tier. Do not try to form groups of equal size; instead, groups should be formed based on the readiness needs of individual students. For example, Tier One may have two groups of three students; Tier Two may have five groups of four students; and Tier Three may have one group of two students. Even if students already are grouped into classes by ability, there is still variability at each ability level, and teachers still need to address these varied ability levels in each population. What you don't want to have happen is that students' tiers differ in the *amount* of work they have to do rather than the *kind* of work they do. Second, be sure each tier is doing moderately challenging and developmentally appropriate work. In other words, no group should be given "busy work." One group should not be doing blackline practice sheets, while another does a fabulous experiment.

Directions for Making Tiered Lessons

According to Adams and Pierce (2006), there are nine steps to developing a tiered lesson.

1. Identify the grade level and subject for which you will write the lesson.
2. Identify the standard (e.g., national, state, and/or local) that you are targeting. A common mistake for those just beginning to tier is to develop three great activities and then try to force them into a tiered lesson. Start with the standard first. If you don't know where you are going, how will you know if you get there?
3. Identify the key concept and essential understanding. The key concept follows from the standard. Ask yourself, "What 'Big Idea' am I targeting?" The essential understanding follows from the concept. Ask yourself, "What do I want the students to know at the end of the lesson, regardless of their placement in the tiers?"
4. Develop a powerful lesson that addresses the essential understanding. This will be the base from which you develop your tiers.
5. Identify the background necessary to complete the lesson and be sure students have this necessary information to be successful in the lesson. What scaffolding is necessary? What must you have already covered or what must the student have already learned? Are there other skills that must be taught first?

6. Determine which element of the lesson you will tier. You may choose to tier the content (what you want the students to learn), the process (the way students make sense out of the content), or the product (the outcome at the end of a lesson, lesson set, or unit—often a project).

7. Determine the readiness of your students. Readiness is based on the ability levels of the students. Preassessing is a good way to determine readiness.

8. Determine how many tiers you will need based on your assessment of the students' readiness to engage in the lesson based on its focus.

9. Determine the appropriate assessment(s) you will use based on your activities. Both formative and summative assessments may be included in the lesson. (pp. 21–22)

How the Strategy Fits in the CIRCLE MAP

Tiered lessons fit in the "differentiated instructional strategies" component of the CIRCLE MAP, as a whole-group activity. Tiered lessons accommodate a variety of readiness levels through whole-class instruction: All students work with the same standard and concept but follow different pathways leading toward the same essential understanding.

Examples

The examples we have chosen include lessons for specific topics and grade levels that may be readily adapted to other grade levels. These lessons were created by real teachers who used them in their own classrooms. When possible, we have included the comments from the teachers and their colleagues with the intention that the comments may provide additional insight into developing your own tiered lessons.

For example, Nick Jackson's AP English class is studying literary analysis. Students have been working on the play *Macbeth* by William Shakespeare. With the help of his mentor, Felicia Dixon, Mr. Jackson creates a lesson that focuses on the application of the archetype of "the fall" as a key to understanding the characters of Macbeth and Lady Macbeth, as well as the actions in this play. This lesson occurs at the end of the reading of Acts I and II of the play. By helping the students focus on an archetype early on, Mr. Jackson helps students gain further insight into the actions of the play and Macbeth's fall that continue after the two initial acts. The difference among the tiers will be the level of critical thinking that must be employed. For example, some students will be working on activities that involve application and analysis, and others will work with synthesis and evaluation activities. While students are working on their activities, Mr. Jackson rotates from group to group to observe student progress and provide assistance as needed.

Template

Title of Tiered Lesson

Subject:

Grade:

Standard(s):

Key Concept:

Essential Understanding:

Background:

Tiered in Content, Process, or Product (choose one)

Tier I:

Tier II:

Tier III:

Assessment:

Literary Analysis: Genocide

Subject: English/Language Arts
Grade: 8 (Honors)

Standards:
- Analyze a work of literature, showing how it reflects the heritage, traditions, attitudes, and beliefs of its author.
- Plan and conduct multistep information searches by using computer networks.
- Write responses to literature that demonstrate careful reading and insight into interpretations.
- Deliver presentations based on research on important ideas, concepts, and direct quotations from significant information sources, and paraphrase and summarize important perspectives on the topic.

Key Concepts: Literary analysis, literature as a means of gaining social understanding

Essential Understanding: Genocide has occurred throughout history. Various social, economic, and government climates can influence the development of such atrocities. It is important that we learn from such horrors so that history cannot repeat itself.

Background: Students will need to understand the terms propaganda, communism, fascism, dictator, and depression (economic). Students will need a brief introduction to how social pressures can cast their influence. Students will also need to know other pertinent geographical and/or historical information.

Tiered in Content

Tier I: As a supplement to their unit on Anne Frank and the Holocaust, students will read the novel *Darfur Diaries: Stories of Survival*, which details the testimonies of those who have survived this atrocity, as well as of those who continue to work to save the people of Darfur.

Tier II: As a supplement to their unit on Anne Frank and the Holocaust, students will read the novel *Three Apples Fell From Heaven*, which recounts a girl's experience in what is known as the Armenian Genocide.

Tier III: As a supplement to their unit on Anne Frank and the Holocaust, students will read the novel *I Have Lived a Thousand Years: Growing Up in the Holocaust*, which recounts the experiences of a Hungarian girl when the Nazis invaded Hungary in 1944.

Assessment: Assessment will be conducted through a variety of means. Students will be responsible for keeping a journal during their reading. The journal will be spot-checked periodically so that I may check for progress and respond to their ideas. In addition, students will be responsible for preparing and participating in literature discussion groups (literature circles) according to their chosen books. Finally, students will be responsible for organizing and completing a "mini-research" presentation on their particular historical example of genocide. They will have to present their information in PowerPoint presentations. (Throughout the research process, various items, such as a source list and a question sheet, will also be collected.) All presentations will be assessed using a rubric that checks for content, effort, amount of information, and so on.

Created by Ami Brown

Real Teacher Comments

I used this with my honors students when we began our work with Anne Frank and the Holocaust. Because I have a small class this year, I was more able to obtain these materials; unfortunately, that wouldn't be the case with a regular-sized group of kids.

This lesson allowed students to see the terrible truth behind the statement "history repeats itself." Although I am an English teacher, I am fascinated with history and its all-too-often predictable patterns. Not only did this give my kids the opportunity to see how such atrocities occur, but it also gave them a larger view of the world in which they live.

—Ami Brown (Teacher)

UNDERSTANDING THEME

Subject: English

Grade: 11/12

Standard: Evaluate the way in which the theme or meaning of a selection represents a view or comments on life, using textual evidence to support the claim.

Key Concept: Theme

Essential Understanding: In discussing themes, readers must be able to go back to the text to find specific examples to support their interpretations.

Background: Previous to this lesson, students would have finished the play *Antony and Cleopatra*. Before reading the play, students did an activity introducing key themes from the play. These themes were occasionally discussed during the play. In this activity, students will be revisiting some of the key themes previously discussed.

Tiered in Content

Tier I: Students in Tier I will be assigned the theme of "honor" (the most straightforward theme of the play). Their first assignment will be to work as a group to come up with an understanding/statement of what message Shakespeare had concerning honor in this play. The teacher will be present for this discussion to help guide students in the right direction. After they have a statement about honor, students will go back to the text to look for examples that illustrate this statement. For the Tier I group, students will be provided with a graphic organizer to record their results. They will also include specific scenes to look to in finding their examples.

Tier II: Students in Tier II will be assigned the theme of "power" (a more challenging, open-ended theme). Their first assignment will be to work as a group to come up with an understanding/statement of what message Shakespeare had concerning power in this play. They will work with only occasional monitoring by the teacher. After they have a statement about power, students will go back to the text to look for examples that illustrate their statement. For the Tier II group, students will be provided with a graphic organizer that asks them to find specific examples related to Caesar, Antony, Cleopatra, and Lepidus. They will not receive help regarding where to find their examples.

Tier III: Students in Tier III will be assigned the theme of "reason versus emotion" (the most abstract, multifaceted of the themes). Their first assignment will be to work as a group to come up with an understanding/statement of what message Shakespeare had concerning reason versus emotion in this play. They will work with only occasional monitoring by the teacher. After they have a statement about reason versus emotion, students will go back to the text to look for examples that illustrate this statement. For the Tier III group, students will be provided with a graphic organizer that provides them room to find examples and properly record them. They will not be given specific guidance regarding where to find these examples or for whom this theme is relevant.

Assessment: Students will receive participation points for turning in their completed group sheets (this will probably take more than one period). This activity will then serve as a springboard for discussion of these themes in following classes. After a class discussion, students will use these same group sheets as a starting point for a literary analysis paper about their assigned theme. The paper will be assessed using a rubric provided when the paper is introduced.

Anchor Activity: All groups will have the opportunity to work on an anchor activity when finished with work in class. They will be asked how their theme relates to present-day society, instructed to find an example in the news that relates to their theme and explain that example, and asked to provide an example from their lives that relates to their theme and explain.

Created by Jenny Duguid

Real Teacher Comments

This is a tiered version of a lesson I've done previously. When I taught this before, the problem I had was that I let students pick the themes they worked on, and I had some who picked themes way over their heads, as well as some who picked themes that were too easy. Doing this as a tiered assignment with assigned groups alleviated that problem and took a lot of the frustration out of this work.

—Jenny Duguid (Teacher)

Literary Devices and Self-Expression

Subject: English

Grade: 10 (Honors)

Standard: Evaluate the significance of various literary devices, including figurative language, imagery, and symbolism, and explain their appeal.

Key Concept: Emotion

Essential Understanding: Students will understand that writing involves self-expression.

Background: Students will already have studied, read, and analyzed poetry, and the uses of figurative language, imagery, and symbolism will have been explained and experimented with through practice exercises.

Tiered in Content

Tier I: Read "Small Portions" by Julia Alvarez. Then select an ordinary object in your home and list its attributes. Write a free verse poem about it from a unique perspective. Include at least one image that appeals to each one of the five senses. Take a picture of the object and attach it to the finished poem.

Tier II: Read "Same Song" by Pat Mora. Think about the people living in your home. Brainstorm a list of unspoken behaviors associated with their daily lives. Write a free verse poem that uses imagery to present one or two of these family members in a poetic light, in which their behaviors/movements are given texture through the senses. Take a picture of these family members and attach it to the finished poem.

Assessment: Formative assessment of the prewriting portion (brainstormed lists); summative assessment of the correct uses/analyses of imagery in the final product.

Created by Stephen Merkle

Real Teacher Comments

I have found that my students are hesitant to put much imagery into their writing unless prompted. I wanted to give them some practice that I thought would be fun for them. By becoming more comfortable with imagery in a more relaxed setting, they might more readily and naturally use imagery without having to be reminded. The students loved the activities, and their free verse was actually quite good. I asked them if it helped them get more comfortable with imagery, and most agreed that it did.

—Stephen Merkle (Teacher)

The Power of Persuasion

Grade Level: 6

Content: Language Arts

Standards:

➤ Use note-taking skills when completing research for writing.

➤ Use organizational features of electronic text (on computers), such as bulletin boards, databases, keyword searches, and e-mail addresses, to locate information.

➤ Use a computer to compose documents with appropriate formatting by using word-processing skills and principles of design, including margins, tabs, spacing, columns, and page orientation.

➤ Write persuasive compositions that:

   ○ State a clear position on a proposition or proposal.

   ○ Support the position with organized and relevant evidence and effective emotional appeals.

   ○ Anticipate and address reader concerns and counterarguments.

   ○ Use varied word choices to make writing interesting.

Key Concept: Persuasion

Essential Understanding: Learning both sides of a topic area can be a powerful way of expressing your own side of an issue.

Background: Students have been introduced to persuasive writing through their language usage books. They have had experience with understanding both sides of a topic.

Tiered in Process

- -

Prior to the activity, the teacher needs to prepare several folders so that each one relates to a current topic and includes materials that address the pros and cons of that topic.

Activity: The persuasive writing activity will be in two tiers. The first tier (photocopied on yellow pages) is for students who are beginning to develop writing analysis and writing skills, but who need more help developing ideas. The second tier (photocopied on blue pages) is for students with more writing analysis and writing experience and skill. All students will complete similar activities, but the activities are tiered according to skill level.

Name:_____ Date:_____

Tier I: You and your partner are practicing for a debate on this topic.

➤ Select a folder of your choice. Open the folder and read the pro and con sides of your topic choice. Highlight three important supporting details for each side. Choose which side you thought did the best job convincing you and write a paragraph explaining the three reasons that convinced you. Explain each reason.

➤ Choose a topic from the list of choices. Read the materials in the folder; highlight the pros and cons of each side. Choose which side did the best job convincing you. Write a paragraph telling why one side or the other did a better job supporting its side of the debate.

➤ Make three note cards to support each side of the topic. Use the note card references to give a reason and supporting details on each note card. Decide which partner will debate for each side. Cards will be used to support your position in a classroom debate.

Tier II:

➤ Read the pro and con sides of your topic choice. Write three pros and three cons for the topic. Choose which side did the best job convincing you. Based on the writings in the Shurley English book, analyze the writings and tell why you believe one side or the other did a better job supporting its side of the debate. Include reasoning on how you would make the other side better.

➤ Choose a topic from the list of choices. Read the materials in that folder, highlight pros and cons of the issue. Choose a side and write a persuasive paragraph supporting the side you have chosen.

➤ Do your own Internet research on the topic. Be sure to take pro and con notes as you read. Write a persuasive essay with three supporting reasons to support your side. Edit and revise the essay using writing materials and forms available in the classroom.

➤ Make note cards supporting your side of the topic you chose for your essay. Be sure to use one card for each supporting reason and detail facts. These cards will be used to support your position in a classroom debate.

Assessment: Written products, response to debate questions, on-time completion, evaluation of debates.

Resources:
➤ Note cards
➤ Internet access
➤ Dictionary
➤ Thesaurus
➤ Shurley English book

Created by Quella Rutledge

Real Teacher Comments

My class is working on persuasive writing. Many of the students have been exposed to debating issues and supporting their positions with factual details, whereas other students have difficulty choosing a position, let alone supporting it with facts. This tiered lesson differentiates for those who are ready to do independent research on high-interest topics and those who need more guidance choosing topics and supporting their positions.

—Quella Rutledge (Teacher)

I really like your lesson. It is very thorough. I could see using a modified version of this with my 10th graders as they work on an editorial. This would work well for inclusion classes with extremely varied ability.

—Jenny (Colleague)

Enriching Nonfiction Writing

Subject: Language Arts

Grade: 8

Standard: Write using precise word choices to make writing interesting and exact.

Key Concept: Words are powerful.

Essential Understanding: Students will understand that effective descriptions are necessary in nonfiction writing as well as in creative writing.

Background: This lesson is part of a unit on "rich writing." We have focused on figurative language, sentence variety, sensory details, and precise adjectives and verbs to make students' writing more vivid and exact. We've practiced and discussed ways to make creative writing richer, but this lesson is a shift towards nonfiction. Students are currently studying the American Civil War in social studies. This assignment will be completed as homework.

Tiered in Product
Tier I: Students will view a clip from the movie *Gettysburg*, which they will access at home via YouTube (covered by release form sent home at the beginning of the year). After viewing the clip, students will assume the role of a reporter and describe the battle using precise and vivid verbs and adjectives, at least two similes/metaphors, and sensory details. The video can be found at http://www.youtube.com/watch?v=zo8u1iP muYc&feature=related (if this video is unavailable, students can watch a different YouTube clip showing a battle from the movie *Gettysburg*).

Tier II: Students will view a QuickTime image of Paul Philippoteaux's Gettysburg Cyclorama. After viewing the picture, students will assume the role of a reporter and describe the battle using precise and vivid verbs and adjectives, at least two similes/metaphors, and sensory details. This image can be found at http://graphics.nytimes.com/packages/html/arts/20051116_GETTY_PANORAMA.html.

Tier III: Students will use knowledge gained about the battle of Gettysburg from social studies class to imagine the battle scene. Students will assume the role of a reporter and describe the battle using precise, vivid verbs and adjectives, at least two similes/metaphors, and sensory details.

Assessment: In class, students will self-assess their writing using a "rich writing" rubric. Students will also compare their writing to the writing of students from the other two tiers and will discuss which technique (film, painting, or imagination) yielded the most vivid description. Finally, the teacher will assess the written descriptions using a rubric.

Created by Lisa Sarjeant

Real Teacher Comments

My eighth graders are in the middle of a "rich writing" unit in which we focus on language precision and effectiveness. I try not to spend too much time on creative writing and poetry in this unit; I want students to see that rich writing is important outside of the English classroom as well (not that I don't love creative writing).

This lesson is about how rich writing can effectively describe and record historical events like battles. It ties into the social studies curriculum, in which students are learning about the Civil War. I want them to describe the Battle of Gettysburg, but as the tiers get higher, students are given fewer sensory clues to help them. Tier 1 gets to see a video clip (visual and auditory), Tier 2 gets a panorama (visual), and Tier 3 has to use only descriptions from their textbooks, relying mostly on their imaginations.

The students produced some great work. I told them from the beginning of the lesson that their assignments were different and that we were going to see which method produced the richest writing. They were fine with that, although they asked if we could all watch the movie clip in class the next day, which I allowed (after the assignments were completed). I think they were surprised to find that some of the Tier 3 descriptions were the most vivid, and we had a great discussion about how your imagination is limitless, whereas if you base your description off of a movie, you are limited to what someone else has already decided you should see. That launched another discussion on accuracy and bias, whether anybody could really write an accurate description of a scene they hadn't witnessed, and so forth. It was a productive discussion and a productive lesson, I thought.

—Lisa Sarjeant (Teacher)

I loved this assignment! Right now in my class we are talking about visualizing poems and what the author was trying to convey. I like the idea of discussing how movies/pictures can alter how we view things. It goes along with the theory that if you read a book first, the movie version is never as good. I think allowing all students to watch the movie the next day was perfect, even if it wasn't planned. It really drove your point home when looking at the different descriptions with fewer sensory clues. I am sure they enjoyed comparing their writing to others' work, especially because they were based on different activities. It's easier to give constructive criticism when the lesson itself was focused on which method gave the richest writing.

—Maura (Colleague)

I definitely plan to take some of your ideas and fit them into my own room. Being able to glean other ideas is amazing!

—Laura (Colleague)

Your idea of using a painting to describe a battle from the point of view of a report sounds interesting. I might apply this idea to my students in their study of colonial America.

—Jeri (Colleague)

The Ladder of Prejudice

The Ladder of Prejudice used in this lesson comes from Gordon W. Allport's (1979) *The Nature of Prejudice*, wherein the author describes a kind of ladder of negative actions that spring from prejudice.

Subject: Prejudice

Grade: Gifted and Talented Grade 7 Language Arts

Standards:
- **Reading: Word Recognition, Fluency, and Vocabulary Development.** Students use their knowledge of word parts and word relationships to determine the meaning of specialized vocabulary.
- **Reading: Comprehension of Literary Texts.** Students read and respond to grade-level-appropriate historically or culturally significant works of literature.
- **Listening and Speaking: Skills, Strategies, and Applications.** Students will deliver focused, coherent presentations that convey ideas clearly and relate to the background and interests of the audience.

Key Concept: Prejudice

Essential Understanding: Students will understand that prejudice manifests itself in many different forms.

Background: This activity will provide the hook for our study of the Holocaust and will set a purpose for reading the novel *The Children of Willesden Lane*, by Mona Golabek and Lee Cohen. Students examine a list of specialized vocabulary words and categorize them. Students develop an understanding of the Ladder of Prejudice and find evidence to support their understanding in historically significant Holocaust literature. The activities will address how *bystanders* and *upstanders* react differently in critical situations, that people do not always become leaders for the right reasons, and how literature offers insights into the condition of the human spirit.

Tiered in Content

Tier I:
- **Part 1:** Students in Tier 1 will be given a partially filled-in Ladder of Prejudice. It will contain the label for each rung of the ladder, 2–3 vocabulary words per rung, and a word bank. Working in small groups, students will fill in the rest of the ladder.
- **Part 2:** Using literature selections from *Voices of the Holocaust*, each group will locate examples that demonstrate students' understanding of the following rungs of the Ladder of Prejudice:
  - o Rung 1–Speech: Treating a group as if all members had one personality, making so-called jokes, name calling, using derogatory terms, and labeling.

  o Rung 2–Avoidance: Having no social interaction with a group, avoiding contact, promoting isolation, and refusing to learn about others.
- **Part 3:** Each group will create a chart, graphic organizer, or collage to demonstrate what it has learned.
- **Part 4:** Each group will present its product to the class.

Tier II:
- **Part 1:** Students in Tier II will be given a partially filled-in Ladder of Prejudice. It will contain the label for each rung of the ladder, one vocabulary word per rung, and a word bank. Working in small groups, students will fill in the rest of the ladder.
- **Part 2:** Using literature selections from *Voices of the Holocaust*, each group will locate examples that demonstrate students' understanding of the following rungs of the Ladder of Prejudice:
  o Rung 3–Discrimination: Groups become targets, group members are kept from social organizations and neighborhoods, and groups are denied rights and privileges.
  o Rung 4–Segregation: Groups are separated and a "Them vs. Us" mentality is taken (e.g., Nazis vs. Jews, Whites vs. Blacks, Asians vs. Hispanics).
- **Part 3:** Each group will create a chart, graphic organizer, or collage to demonstrate what it has learned.
- **Part 4:** Each group will present its product to the class.

Tier III:
- **Part 1:** Students in Tier III will be given a Ladder of Prejudice. It will contain the label for each rung of the ladder and a word bank. Working in small groups, students will fill in the rest of the ladder.
- **Part 2:** Using literature selections from *Voices of the Holocaust*, each group will locate examples that demonstrate students' understanding of the following rungs of the Ladder of Prejudice:
  o Rung 5–Physical Attack: Mob violence, gang violence, property damage, and personal assaults are committed.
  o Rung 6–Extermination: Lynching, massacre, genocide, assassination, and murder are committed.
- **Part 3:** Each group will create a chart, graphic organizer, or collage to demonstrate what it has learned.
- **Part 4:** Each group will present its product to the class.

Assessment: Students will be assessed using Group Participation, Project, and Oral Presentation rubrics.

Created by Susan Schweitzer

Real Teacher Comments

This tiered lesson on prejudice will function as the hook for my unit on the Holocaust. Its purpose is to allow students to examine specialized vocabulary, to understand the Ladder of Prejudice, and to locate examples in literature to demonstrate their understanding of these concepts. When my students have completed tiered activities in the past, they were eye-opening experiences. I found that students were more engaged in their learning because the activities were designed at appropriate readiness levels. Activities that allow students to work at their appropriate levels create a win-win situation.

—Susan Schweitzer (Teacher)

I like that all of your students were working on the same thing with varying degrees of scaffolding. I also liked that they all got the opportunity to present their findings—no one should feel left out or singled out by your lesson.

—Jennifer (Colleague)

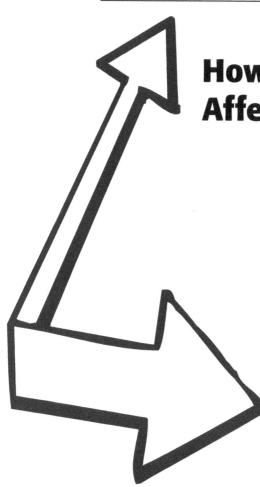

How a Character's Actions Affect a Story

Subject: Language Arts

Grade: 6

Standards:
- Identify different types (genres) of fiction and describe the major characteristics of each.
- Analyze the effects of the qualities of the character on the plot and the resolution of the conflict.
- Identify and analyze features of themes conveyed through characters, actions, and images.

Key Concept: Cause and effect

Essential Understanding: Students should understand how the attributes and actions of characters are essential to developing an understanding of the underlying message in the story.

Background: Students have studied vocabulary words defining a folk tale, the four main types of folk tales (fables, myths, legends, and tall tales), a stereotype, a cultural value, and a universal theme. They took notes on characteristics of folk tales and discussed their origins, purposes, and importance to a culture. Students have studied various fables and are familiar with identifying very simple lessons.

Tiered in Product

Students will use the selection "Apollo's Tree" in their textbooks.

Tier I: After reading and discussing the myth together, **students will receive a cause and effect chart with major events from the story in which each box is the result of the box before it and the cause of the box after it**. This will help them see how the characters' actions affect what happens in the story. They will use this information to answer specific questions about the theme or the lesson of the story and its importance to the culture of the story.

Tier II: After reading and discussing the myth together, students will receive a cause and effect chart with major events from the story in which each box is the result of the box before it and the cause of the box after it. **Several boxes will be blank, and students will be expected**

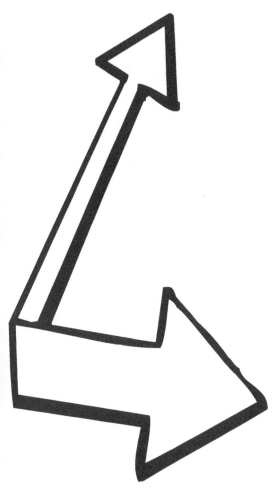

to complete them with the appropriate information. This will help them see how the characters' actions affect what happens in the story. They can use this information to write a paragraph in which they give the major theme of the story and support their answer by explaining how the characters' actions lead to Daphne's and Apollo's disastrous end.

Tier III: After reading and discussing the myth together, **students will receive a blank cause and effect chart, which they must complete with major events from the story**. This will help them see how the characters' actions affect what happens in the story. They can use this information to write a paragraph in which they give the major theme of the story and support their answer by explaining how the characters' actions lead to Daphne's and Apollo's disastrous end.

Select an appropriate chart from http://www.educationoasis.com/curriculum/GO/cause_effect.htm

Assessment: Students will be assessed on completing their cause and effect charts with accurate events, as well as on their use of the information to support their explanation of the story's message.

Created by Tracy Schwerin

Real Teacher Comments

My students really enjoyed this activity because they love to read folk tales. I wanted to use a graphic organizer, so I picked a cause and effect chart for each tier. I modified my chart based on the students' readiness by providing more scaffolding with the Tier I students and less with Tier III. I was amazed at how well they responded and demonstrated their knowledge. Their ability to pick out supporting information was much improved.

—Tracy Schwerin (Teacher)

The Effect of Point of View

Subject: Language Arts

Grade: 7

Standards:
- Identify and trace the development of an author's argument, point of view, or perspective in text.
- Contrast points of view—first person, third person, limited, omniscient, subjective, objective—in a literary text and explain how each affects the overall theme of the work.

Key Concepts:
- Comparison and contrast
- Point of view

Essential Understanding: Changes in narrator and point of view change how we understand the story. The students will be able to list similarities and differences between two stories. Finding similarities and differences between two stories helps us gain a greater understanding of the stories.

Background: We are doing a unit on point of view and types of narration. The students have already been exposed to first person, third person, and omniscient narrators. They have enough information that this activity should be able to be completed independently, in pairs, or in small groups.

As review, either read aloud the story of Cinderella or have it available for those who may need it.

Tiered in Content

Tier I: Read "Dinorella" by Pamela Duncan Edwards in partners. Complete the activities listed on the next page.

Tier II: Read "Yeh-Shen," retold by Ai-Ling Louie, in partners. Complete the activities listed on the next page.

Tier III: Read "Aschenputtel," retold by Jakob and Wilhelm Grimm. Complete the activities listed below.

Activity: Students will create a Venn diagram comparing and contrasting their readings with the traditional version of *Cinderella*. Similarities and differences should appear in the diagram.

Students will create a list of what would change in their assigned story if it were told from another character's point of view (e.g., the stepmother's).

The lists and diagrams will be turned in at the end of class. A class discussion will take place the next day to discuss all three stories so that all students can present what they learned.

Next, students will meet in groups based on which characters they chose for the new points of view. They will compare the lists they made, come to a consensus on the five most important changes in they story, and share their results with rest of the class.

Created by Teri Vasquez

Real Teacher Comments

The students either worked in pairs or independently on this project based on their readiness level. At first they were shocked that we were going to read three different short stories. They had done this before with complete novels, but not as much for short stories. I tried to make it appear that I was using a pattern when I assigned the stories. I think that at the middle school level, kids are really sensitive about sticking out. If I called all the lower ability kids out first and all the upper ability kids out last, they would know that I was assigning the story based on ability. I think the pattern fixed that problem.

—Teri Vasquez (Teacher)

I agree with you about the sensitivity of middle school (and high school) students. They are quick to pick up on who is in the "slow" group if you aren't careful. It sounds like your pattern technique worked well. This is also something that I have to be really sensitive about in my inclusion English classes. I have students ranging from MIMH to twice-exceptional students, those who are gifted and who also have a learning disability. Even lower functioning students are wary of the "low" group, so it takes some creative wording and selling of activities to get them to look past this. I think this really points out the importance of using the differentiation mindset at all times. Then students know you are always trying to find the best placement for them for any given activity.

—Jenny (Colleague)

REFERENCES

Adams, C. M., & Pierce, R. L. (2006). *Differentiating instruction: A practical guide to tiering lessons in the elementary grades.* Waco, TX: Prufrock Press.

Allport, G. W. (1979). *The nature of prejudice.* New York, NY: Perseus Books.

Coil, C. (2007). *Successful teaching in the differentiated classroom.* Marion, IL: Pieces of Learning.

Erickson, H. L. (2002). *Concept-based curriculum and instruction.* Thousand Oaks, CA: Corwin Press.

Gregory, G. H., & Chapman, C. (2002). *Differentiated instructional strategies: One size doesn't fit all.* Thousand Oaks, CA: Corwin Press.

Kingore, B. (2004). *Differentiation: Simplified, realistic, and effective.* Austin, TX: Professional Associates.

Passow, A. H. (1982). *Differentiated curricula for the gifted/talented: A point of view.* Ventura, CA: Ventura County Superintendent of Schools Office.

Tomlinson, C. A. (1999). *The differentiated classroom: Responding to the needs of all learners.* Alexandria, VA: ASCD.

Tomlinson, C. A. (2001). *How to differentiate instruction in mixed-ability classrooms* (2nd ed.). Alexandria, VA: ASCD.

Tomlinson, C. A. (2003). *Fulfilling the promise of the differentiated classroom.* Alexandria, VA: ASCD.

Ward, V. (1980). *Differential education for the gifted.* Ventura, CA: National/State Leadership Training Institute for the Gifted and Talented.

Winebrenner, S. A. (1992). *Teaching gifted kids in the regular classroom: Strategies and techniques every teacher can use to meet the academic needs of the gifted and talented.* Minneapolis, MN: Free Spirit.

ABOUT THE AUTHORS

Cheryll M. Adams is the director of the Center for Gifted Studies and Talent Development at Ball State University. She teaches graduate courses for the license in gifted education. For the past 30 years, she has served in the field of gifted education as a teacher of gifted students at all grade levels, director of Academic Life at the Indiana Academy for Science, Mathematics, and Humanities, and as the principal teacher in the Ball State Institute for the Gifted in Mathematics program. Additionally, she has been the founder and director of various other programs for gifted students. Dr. Adams has authored or coauthored numerous publications in professional journals, as well as several book chapters. She serves on the editorial review board for *Roeper Review*, *Gifted Child Quarterly*, *Journal for the Education of the Gifted*, and *The Teacher Educator*. She has served on the Board of Directors of the National Association for Gifted Children, has been president of the Indiana Association for the Gifted, and currently serves as president of The Association for the Gifted, Council for Exceptional Children. In 2002 she received the NAGC Early Leader Award.

Rebecca L. Pierce is associate professor of mathematical sciences at Ball State University and fellow at the Center for Gifted Studies and Talent Development. She teaches undergraduate and graduate courses in mathematics and statistics. For the last 35 years, Dr. Pierce has taught mathematics to elementary, middle school, high school, and college students. Dr. Pierce directs the Ball State Institute for the Gifted in Mathematics. Additionally, she worked as a Senior Research Engineer for Bell Helicopter and as a statistical consultant for a variety of industries. She has authored or coauthored numerous publications in professional journals, as well as several book chapters. She is the chair of Mathematics Day, a program for middle school girls interested in mathematics. She serves as a reviewer for *Roeper Review*, *Gifted Child Quarterly*, *Journal for the Education of the Gifted*, and *The Teacher*

Educator. She received the Leadership Award from the Indiana Association for the Gifted in 2002.

Dr. Adams and Dr. Pierce work with teachers throughout the United States and Europe toward establishing more effectively differentiated classrooms through the use of the CIRCLE MAP. In addition, they provide professional development and consultation in the areas of mathematics, science, identification, and program evaluation. They have coauthored and received three Javits grants from the federal government in partnership with the Indiana schools.